LOYALTY
IN EVERYTHING

A GUIDE TO BUILDING STRONG

RELATIONSHIPS IN BUSINESS AND LIFE

WRITTEN BY "LOYALTY" CASSANDRA MITCHELL

LOYALTY IN EVERYTHING

LOYALTY IN EVERTHING:
A GUIDE TO BUILDING STRONG RELATIONSHIPS IN BUSINESS AND LIFE
Copyright © 2023 by "LOYALTY " CASSANDRA MITCHELL

The images used in this book are taken from canvas.com

All rights reserved. No part of this book may be reproduced or transmitted in any form or by any means without written permission from the author.

ISBN:979-8-9887748-0-8

DEDICATION PAGE

TO MY DEAR FRIENDS AND FAMILY

Chief Executive Officer

This book is dedicated to you, who have been a constant source of loyalty and support throughout my life. Your unwavering presence in my personal and professional life has been invaluable.

The concept of loyalty has always been a guiding principle in my life, and I am grateful for the lessons you have taught me about what it truly means to be loyal. Your loyalty has inspired me to write this book, which is a guide to building strong relationships in both business and life.

I hope that insights shared in this book will serve as a tribute to the loyalty and love you have shown me over the years. Thank you for always being there, for your encouragement, and for your unwavering support.

With love and gratitude,

"Loyalty"
Cassandra Mitchell

Dedicated to excellence

TABLE OF CONTENTS

01. The Power of Loyalty
02. Building Trust Through Loyalty
03. The Benefits of Loyalty in Business
04. Navigating Loyalty in Professional Relationships
05. Balancing Loyalty and Self-Interest
06. The Role of Communication in Loyalty
07. The Challenges of Loyalty in Personal Relationships
08. Overcoming Betrayal and Rebuilding Loyalty
09. Teaching Loyalty to the Next Generation
10. Loyalty in the Digital Age

TABLE OF CONTENTS

11. The Dark Side of Loyalty
12. Loyalty as a Two-Way Street
13. Balancing Loyalty and Diversity
14. The Future of Loyalty
15. Loyalty In Crisis
16. The Intersection of Loyalty and Ethics
17. Loyalty In Leadership
18. Loyalty in Family Dynamics
19. The Psychology of Loyalty
20. Cultivating Loyalty through Gratitude

FOREWORD

By Terecka Brown

As an Accountability Coach, I have had the opportunity to work with individuals and organizations from various industries and backgrounds. One thing that I have consistently seen as a key factor in building successful relationships, both in business and in life, is loyalty. Loyalty can be defined as a strong feeling of support or allegiance, and it is an essential element that contributes to the growth and success of any relationship.

In "Loyalty in Everything: A Guide to Building Strong Relationships in Business and Life," author Cassandra Mitchell, also known as Loyalty, provides an insightful and practical guide to help readers cultivate loyalty in all aspects of their lives. Cassandra draws upon her years of experience working in the corporate world, as well as her personal relationships, to provide readers with practical tips and advice on how to build and maintain strong relationships.

"Loyalty in everything is a rare and precious trait that should be cherished and celebrated. It speaks volumes about a person's character and their commitment to their beliefs and values."

#LoyaltyInEverything

FOREWORD CONTINUED

Throughout the pages of this book, readers will learn about the importance of communication, trust, and respect in building strong relationships. They will also gain a deeper understanding of how to identify and manage toxic relationships and how to develop a strong support system that will help them navigate life's challenges.

What I appreciate most about "Loyalty in Everything" is that it is not just a theoretical guide. Cassandra provides real-life examples and practical strategies that readers can apply immediately to their personal and professional relationships. Whether you are a business owner, an employee, or simply someone who wants to build stronger relationships, this book is a must-read.

Loyalty In Everything

"To have loyalty in everything means to remain steadfast and unwavering in your dedication to your relationships, your work, and your passions. It requires patience, perseverance, and a deep sense of responsibility to the things that matter most in your life."

FOREWORD CONTINUED

As you embark on your journey to build stronger relationships, I encourage you to approach this book with an open mind and a willingness to learn. You will undoubtedly walk away with a renewed sense of purpose and a deeper understanding of what it takes to cultivate loyalty in everything you do.

Terecka Brown
Accountability Coach

traitorous,
loyalty *n.*
never wa

INTRODUCTION

In our fast-paced world, building and maintaining strong relationships can be a challenge. Whether it's in our personal or professional lives, we are often faced with the pressure to constantly be on the move, to always look for the next best thing, and to prioritize our own interests over those of others. However, there is one powerful trait that can help us overcome these challenges and foster long-lasting, meaningful relationships: loyalty.

In "Loyalty In Everything: A Guide to Building Strong Relationships in Business and Life," we explore the importance of loyalty and how it can help us navigate the complexities of modern life. Through a combination of real-world examples, practical advice, and thought-provoking insights, this book provides a roadmap for anyone looking to cultivate deeper connections with the people around them.

Whether you are a business leader looking to build a loyal customer base, an individual seeking to strengthen your personal relationships, or simply someone interested in exploring the power of loyalty, this book is for you. By the end of this journey, you will have a newfound appreciation for the role that loyalty plays in our lives, and a set of practical tools to help you cultivate it in everything you do.

CHAPTER 1
The Power of Loyalty

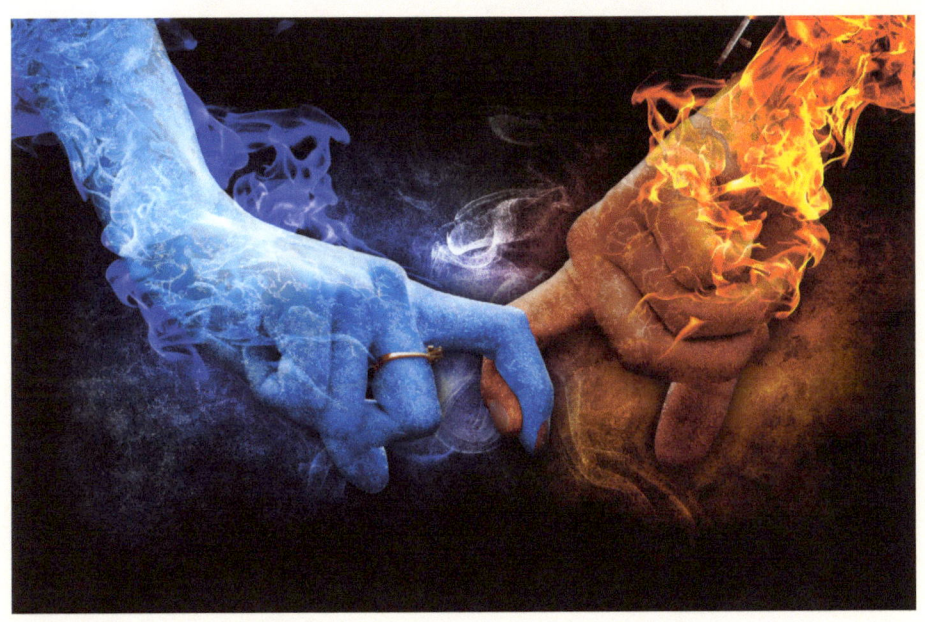

"Loyalty is the foundation upon which strong relationships are built, whether in business or in life."

#LOYALTYINEVERYTHING

CHAPTER 1
The Power of Loyalty

Introduction

Loyalty is a virtue that has been valued throughout history. It is an essential component of strong relationships, whether personal or professional. Loyalty can be defined as a strong feeling of commitment or allegiance towards someone or something. It involves being faithful, dependable, and supportive, even in difficult times.

In this chapter, we will explore the power of loyalty and its importance in building strong relationships. We will discuss some examples of loyalty in action, the benefits of loyalty in personal and professional life, the connection between loyalty and trust, and how to cultivate loyalty in yourself and others.

The Importance of Loyalty in Building Strong Relationships

Loyalty is an essential component of building strong relationships. Whether it is a romantic relationship, a friendship, or a professional relationship, loyalty is crucial to its success. When people are loyal, they are committed to the relationship and willing to work through any challenges that may arise. Loyalty helps to build trust, which is critical in any relationship. Without trust, a relationship cannot thrive.

One of the benefits of loyalty is that it creates a sense of security. When people know that someone is loyal to them, they feel safe and secure in the relationship. They know that they can count on their partner, friend, or colleague to be there for them, no matter what. This sense of security helps to strengthen the bond between people and makes the relationship more meaningful.

THE POWER OF LOYALTY

Examples of Loyalty In Action

There are countless examples of loyalty in action. One of the most famous examples is that of Ruth and Naomi in the Bible. Ruth was loyal to her mother-in-law, Naomi, even after her husband died. She refused to leave Naomi's side, saying, "Where you go I will go, and where you stay I will stay. Your people will be my people and your God my God" (Ruth 1:16).

Another example of loyalty is that of Jonathan and David in the Bible. Jonathan was the son of King Saul, and David was a young shepherd whom God had anointed as the future king of Israel. Despite the fact that Jonathan's father was trying to kill David, Jonathan remained loyal to him. He helped David to escape and even made a covenant with him, saying, "May the Lord call David's enemies to account" (1 Samuel 20:16).

In more recent times, there are countless examples of loyalty in action. One such example is that of Jim Lovell and his crew during the Apollo 13 mission. When their spacecraft suffered a catastrophic malfunction, the crew worked together to overcome the odds and make it back to Earth safely. Their loyalty to each other helped to save their lives.

Loyalty has numerous benefits in both personal and professional life. In personal life, loyalty helps to build strong relationships. It creates a sense of security and trust, which makes the relationship more meaningful. When people know that someone is loyal to them, they are more likely to be loyal in return, which helps to strengthen the bond between them.

THE POWER OF LOYALTY

In professional life, loyalty is also essential. When employees are loyal to their company, they are more committed to their work and more likely to go above and beyond to ensure the company's success. This, in turn, leads to higher productivity and better business outcomes.

Loyal employees are also more likely to stay with a company for the long term. This helps to reduce turnover, which can be costly for businesses. Additionally, loyal employees are more likely to recommend their company to others, which can help to attract top talent between people and makes the relationship more meaningful.

The Connection Between Loyalty and Trust

Loyalty and trust are closely connected. When people are loyal, they are committed to the relationship and willing to work through any challenges that may arise. This commitment helps to build trust between people. When people trust each other, they feel comfortable being vulnerable and sharing their thoughts and feelings. This, in turn, strengthens the bond between them and makes the relationship more meaningful.

Trust is also essential in professional relationships. When employees trust their employer, they are more likely to be committed to their work and willing to go above and beyond to ensure the company's success. Additionally, customers are more likely to trust companies that they perceive as being loyal to their customers. This can lead to increased customer loyalty and higher levels of customer satisfaction.

THE POWER OF LOYALTY

How To Cultivate Loyalty In Yourself And Others

Cultivating loyalty in yourself and others is essential for building strong relationships. Here are some tips for cultivating loyalty:

1. Be trustworthy: The first step in cultivating loyalty is to be trustworthy. When people trust you, they are more likely to be loyal to you.

2. Show loyalty: If you want others to be loyal to you, you need to show loyalty to them. This means being there for them when they need you and being committed to the relationship.

3. Communicate openly: Communication is key to building strong relationships. Be open and honest with others and encourage them to do the same with you.

4. Be reliable: Being reliable is essential for building trust and loyalty. If you say you are going to do something, follow through on your commitment.

5. Show appreciation: People are more likely to be loyal to you if they feel appreciated. Take the time to show gratitude for the people in your life.

6. Be supportive: Being supportive of others is another way to cultivate loyalty. Offer your support when someone is going through a difficult time, and be there to celebrate their successes.

7. Build shared experiences: Shared experiences can help to strengthen the bond between people. Take the time to create memories with the people in your life.

THE POWER OF LOYALTY

Conclusion

Loyalty is a powerful virtue that is essential for building strong relationships. It creates a sense of security and trust, which makes the relationship more meaningful. Cultivating loyalty in yourself and others is essential for building strong relationships, both personal and professional. By being trustworthy, showing loyalty, communicating openly, being reliable, showing appreciation, being supportive, and building shared experiences, you can cultivate loyalty and build stronger relationships.

Loyalty is about being honest, trustworthy, and true to your word.

LOYALTY IN EVERYTHING: A GUIDE TO BUILDING STRONG RELATIONSHIPS IN BUSINESS AND LIFE

Through Loyalty we build trust...

#LOYALTYINEVERYTHING

CHAPTER 2
Building Trust through Loyalty

"IN A WORLD OF CHANGING TIDES, LOYALTY REMAINS THE ANCHOR THAT HOLDS RELATIONSHIPS STEADY."

#LOYALTYINEVERYTHING

CHAPTER 2
Building Trust through Loyalty

Introduction

Trust is a key component in any relationship, whether it is personal or professional. Without trust, relationships cannot thrive, as they lack the necessary foundation for growth and development. Trust is built over time through various means, including honesty, reliability, and empathy. Loyalty is one of the most critical aspects of building trust, as it demonstrates a commitment to the relationship and creates a sense of safety and security between people. In this chapter, we will explore the role of trust in relationships and how loyalty builds trust. We will also examine the importance of trust in personal and professional relationships, as well as strategies for building and maintaining trust through loyalty.

The Role of Trust in Relationships

Trust is a crucial element in building strong relationships. It is a foundational element that allows people to be vulnerable and open with each other, leading to deeper connections and more meaningful relationships. Trust creates a sense of safety and security, which allows people to rely on one another and build a sense of community. Without trust, relationships can become superficial, lacking depth and meaning.

In personal relationships, trust allows people to share their innermost thoughts, feelings, and desires with their partners, friends, and family members. Trust creates an environment where people can be themselves without fear of judgment or rejection. Trust also allows people to form

BUILDING TRUST THROUGH LOYALTY

bonds that are based on mutual respect and understanding, which is critical in developing strong, healthy relationships.

In professional relationships, trust is equally important. Trust allows employees to feel secure in their work environment and to trust their colleagues, managers, and employers. Trust also promotes teamwork, collaboration, and productivity, as employees are more likely to work together effectively when they trust one another. Trust is also critical in building a positive reputation for a company, as customers are more likely to do business with a company that they trust.

How Loyalty Builds Trust

Loyalty is a key component in building trust. Loyalty is demonstrated through actions that show a commitment to the relationship, such as being there for someone during difficult times, following through on promises, and supporting someone's goals and aspirations. Loyalty creates a sense of safety and security, as it shows that someone is committed to the relationship and can be relied upon.

When someone demonstrates loyalty, it creates a positive feedback loop that builds trust. For example, if a friend stands by you during a difficult time, you are more likely to trust them in the future. This trust is built on the foundation of loyalty, as it shows that the friend is committed to the relationship and has your best interests at heart. Over time, this loyalty and trust can lead to a deeper, more meaningful friendship.

BUILDING TRUST THROUGH LOYALTY

Similarly, in a professional setting, when an employee demonstrates loyalty to their employer by going above and beyond to ensure the success of the company, they are building trust with their employer. This trust is built on the foundation of loyalty, as it shows that the employee is committed to the success of the company and can be relied upon to work hard and contribute to the company's growth.

Examples of How Trust is Developed Through Loyalty

There are many examples of how trust is developed through loyalty. For example, if a spouse is loyal to their partner, they demonstrate their commitment to the relationship. This loyalty can lead to increased trust, as the partner feels secure in the relationship and believes that their spouse has their best interests at heart. Over time, this trust can lead to a deeper, more meaningful relationship.

Similarly, in a professional setting, when an employee is loyal to their employer, they demonstrate their commitment to the company's success. This loyalty can lead to increased trust, as the employer feels secure in the knowledge that the employee is dedicated to the company and its goals. Over time, this trust can lead to a more productive and successful working relationship.

BUILDING TRUST THROUGH LOYALTY

The importance of trust in personal and professional relationships

Trust is a fundamental aspect of any relationship, be it personal or professional. It is the foundation upon which strong connections are built, and without it, relationships may be shallow and unsatisfying. Trust allows individuals to feel safe and secure, and to rely on others for support and guidance. In this section, we will explore the importance of trust in personal and professional relationships and how it impacts individuals and organizations.

In personal relationships, trust plays a crucial role in building intimacy, vulnerability, and a sense of belonging. When we trust our loved ones, we feel comfortable being ourselves, expressing our emotions, and sharing our deepest fears and hopes. Trust allows us to feel safe in our relationships, which fosters a sense of security and comfort. Moreover, trust helps us to communicate effectively and to work through conflicts and disagreements that are an inevitable part of any relationship.

In contrast, a lack of trust in personal relationships can create feelings of suspicion, doubt, and insecurity. Without trust, individuals may feel reluctant to share their feelings, fearing that they will be judged or rejected. This can lead to misunderstandings, resentment, and ultimately, the breakdown of the relationship. In the absence of trust, it can be challenging to build a strong and lasting connection with someone, which is why it is so critical to establish trust in personal relationships.

BUILDING TRUST THROUGH LOYALTY

Similarly, trust plays a vital role in professional relationships as well. In the workplace, trust helps to create a positive and productive work environment, where individuals feel comfortable working together towards common goals. When employees trust their colleagues and managers, they are more likely to collaborate, share information, and work towards the greater good of the organization. This leads to increased productivity, job satisfaction, and employee retention.

Moreover, trust is essential in building a strong reputation for the organization. Customers are more likely to do business with a company that they trust, as they feel confident that their needs will be met and their interests will be protected. Trust is, therefore, critical in building long-term relationships with customers, which is essential for the success of any organization.

In conclusion, trust is a fundamental aspect of both personal and professional relationships. It creates a sense of safety, security, and belonging, allowing individuals to be themselves and to build strong connections with others. Trust is essential in building a positive and productive work environment, where employees feel comfortable collaborating and working towards common goals. Moreover, trust is essential in building a strong reputation for the organization and in building long-term relationships with customers. Without trust, relationships can be shallow and unsatisfying, leading to feelings of doubt, suspicion, and insecurity. Therefore, it is critical to establish and maintain trust in both personal and professional relationships for the betterment of individuals and organizations.

BUILDING TRUST THROUGH LOYALTY

Professional Relationships

Trust is important in both personal and professional relationships. In personal relationships, trust allows people to be vulnerable and open with each other, which can lead to deeper, more meaningful connections. Trust also creates a sense of safety and security, which allows people to rely on one another and build a sense of community. Without trust, personal relationships can become superficial, lacking depth and meaning.

In professional relationships, trust is equally important. Trust allows employees to feel secure in their work environment and to trust their colleagues, managers, and employers. This can lead to increased productivity, as employees are more likely to work together effectively when they trust one another. Trust is also critical in building a positive reputation for a company, as customers are more likely to do business with a company that they trust.

How to Build Trust Through Loyalty

Building trust through loyalty requires a concerted effort to demonstrate a commitment to the relationship. Here are some strategies for building trust through loyalty:

1. Be reliable: One of the most important aspects of building trust through loyalty is being reliable. Follow through on promises and commitments, and be there for others when they need you.

BUILDING TRUST THROUGH LOYALTY

2. Show empathy: Demonstrating empathy can help build trust in personal relationships. Show understanding and compassion for others' feelings and experiences, and be there to support them when they need it.

3. Be honest: Honesty is a crucial component in building trust. Be honest with yourself and others, and do not hide your true feelings or intentions.

4. Communicate openly: Communication is key in building trust. Be open and transparent in your communication, and listen actively to others' perspectives.

5. Be consistent: Consistency is important in building trust. Act in a way that is consistent with your values and beliefs, and be reliable in your actions and commitments.

Maintaining Trust Through Loyalty

Maintaining trust through loyalty requires ongoing effort and commitment. Here are some strategies for maintaining trust through loyalty:

1. Be transparent: Transparency is key in maintaining trust. Be open and honest about your actions and intentions, and communicate openly with others.

2. Follow through on commitments: Follow through on your commitments, and be reliable in your actions and behaviors. This can help maintain trust over time.

BUILDING TRUST THROUGH LOYALTY

3. Show empathy: Showing empathy can help maintain trust in personal relationships. Show understanding and compassion for others' feelings and experiences, and be there to support them when they need it.

4. Communicate regularly: Regular communication is important in maintaining trust. Stay in touch with others, and keep them informed about your actions and intentions.

5. Be consistent: Consistency is important in maintaining trust. Act in a way that is consistent with your values and beliefs, and be reliable in your actions and commitments.

Conclusion

Trust is a crucial component in building strong relationships, both personal and professional. Loyalty is a key factor in building trust, as it demonstrates a commitment to the relationship and creates a sense of safety and security between people. Through loyalty, trust can be built over time, leading to deeper, more meaningful relationships. By being reliable, honest, empathetic, communicative, and consistent, trust can be built and maintained over time, leading to stronger, more resilient relationships.

CHAPTER 3
The Benefits of Loyalty in Business

"TRUE LOYALTY MEANS STANDING BY SOMEONE'S SIDE THROUGH BOTH THE SUNNY DAYS AND THE STORMY NIGHTS."

#LoyaltyInEverything

THE BENEFITS OF LOYALTY IN BUSINESS

Leadership plays a crucial role in creating a culture of loyalty in the workplace. Leaders who are approachable, supportive, and empathetic are more likely to build trust and loyalty among their employees. They should be willing to listen to employee feedback and make changes based on that feedback. Leaders who lead by example and demonstrate a commitment to the company's values and mission are also more likely to inspire loyalty among their employees.

The Connection between Loyalty and Profitability

Loyalty is directly connected to profitability. Companies with loyal customers and employees are more likely to have higher levels of revenue and profitability. Loyal customers are more likely to make repeat purchases, provide positive word-of-mouth referrals, and be less price-sensitive. This can lead to increased revenue and profitability for the company.

Loyal employees also have a direct impact on profitability. They are more productive, knowledgeable, and engaged, which can lead to increased efficiency and higher levels of customer satisfaction. This, in turn, can lead to increased revenue and profitability for the company.

Conclusion

Loyalty is a critical factor in the success of any business. It leads to customer and employee retention, improved customer satisfaction, and increased profitability. Building a loyal customer base requires a strategic and ongoing effort that involves understanding customer needs and preferences, providing excellent customer service, rewarding

THE BENEFITS OF LOYALTY IN BUSINESS

loyalty, and a commitment to continuous improvement. Creating a culture of loyalty in the workplace requires a commitment to employee satisfaction and engagement, clear communication, and leadership that inspires trust and loyalty. Companies that prioritize loyalty are more likely to achieve long-term success and profitability.

CHAPTER 4
Navigating Loyalty in Professional Relationships

"A loyal heart is a precious gem, rare and invaluable in any relationship."

#LoyaltyInEverything

CHAPTER 4
Navigating Loyalty in Professional Relationships

Introduction

In any workplace, loyalty plays a crucial role in building and maintaining professional relationships. Employees who are loyal to their colleagues, superiors, and the organization they work for tend to foster a positive work environment that promotes teamwork, trust, and cooperation. However, navigating loyalty in the workplace can be challenging, and striking a balance between loyalty and self-interest can be difficult. In this chapter, we will explore the importance of loyalty in professional relationships, the challenges it presents, and the benefits it offers.

The Importance of Loyalty in Professional Relationships

Loyalty is an essential aspect of any professional relationship. It refers to a commitment to stand by someone or something even when faced with challenging situations or adversity. In the workplace, loyalty involves being supportive of colleagues and superiors, promoting their interests, and being willing to go the extra mile to help them succeed. When employees are loyal, they tend to be more committed to their work, which can result in higher productivity, job satisfaction, and overall performance.

NAVIGATING LOYALY IN PROFESSIONAL RELATIONSHIPS

Loyal employees are also more likely to build and maintain positive relationships with their colleagues and superiors. These relationships are essential in promoting a positive work environment that fosters collaboration, communication, and teamwork. When employees are loyal, they tend to be more willing to work together and support one another, which can help to create a more cohesive and productive team.

The Challenges of Loyalty in the Workplace

While loyalty is important, it can also be challenging to navigate in the workplace. One of the primary challenges of loyalty is balancing it with self-interest. Employees must find a way to be loyal to their colleagues and superiors while also ensuring their own success and advancement. This can be difficult, as it requires finding a balance between promoting others' interests and advancing one's career.

Another challenge of loyalty is maintaining it in the face of competition. In the workplace, employees may feel pressure to be loyal to one colleague or superior over another, particularly if they are competing for the same job or promotion. This can be challenging, as employees may feel torn between supporting one person or another. In such cases, it is essential to maintain a sense of fairness and objectivity and to avoid taking sides or showing favoritism.

Balancing Loyalty and Self-Interest

One of the keys to navigating loyalty in the workplace is finding a way to balance it with self-interest. Employees must find a way to be loyal to their colleagues and superiors while also advancing their own careers and interests. This can be achieved by being supportive of others while also being proactive in pursuing one's own goals and aspirations.

NAVIGATING LOYALY IN PROFESSIONAL RELATIONSHIPS

To maintain loyalty in the face of competition, employees must remain objective and fair. This means avoiding taking sides or showing favoritism and being willing to recognize and support the contributions and accomplishments of all colleagues and superiors, regardless of personal preferences. Additionally, employees can maintain loyalty by focusing on their own work and performance, rather than getting caught up in office politics or gossip.

The Benefits of Loyal Professional Relationships

Loyal professional relationships offer a range of benefits, both for individual employees and the organization as a whole. Some of these benefits include:

1. Increased productivity: Loyal employees tend to be more committed to their work, which can result in higher levels of productivity and performance.

2. Positive work environment: Loyal employees help to create a positive work environment that promotes teamwork, trust, and collaboration.

3. Stronger relationships: Loyal employees tend to build stronger relationships with their colleagues and superiors, which can help to promote communication and collaboration.

4. Greater job satisfaction: Loyal employees are more likely to be satisfied with their jobs, as they feel valued and supported by their colleagues and superiors.

5. Better retention rates: Organizations that foster loyal professional relationships are more likely to retain their employees, as they are committed to the company and its goals.

NAVIGATING LOYALY IN PROFESSIONAL RELATIONSHIPS

Conclusion

Loyalty is a crucial aspect of any professional relationship, and navigating it in the workplace can be challenging. Employees must find a way to balance loyalty with self-interest, build and maintain loyal relationships with their colleagues and superiors, and remain objective and fair in the face of competition. However, the benefits of loyal professional relationships are significant, and organizations that prioritize loyalty are more likely to foster a positive work environment that promotes collaboration, communication, and productivity.

CHAPTER 5
Balancing Loyalty and Self-Interest

"Loyalty is not blind allegiance; it's a conscious choice to stay committed to what truly matters."

#LOYALTYINEVERYTHING

CHAPTER 5
Balancing Loyalty and Self-Interest

Introduction

Loyalty and self-interest are two powerful forces that can often conflict with one another. On one hand, loyalty is a virtue that is valued in personal and professional relationships. It is a sense of devotion and commitment that one has towards another person or group. On the other hand, self-interest is the concern for one's own well-being and personal goals. In many situations, balancing these two forces can be a difficult task, and failure to do so can result in negative consequences.

The Importance of Balancing Loyalty and Self-Interest

Balancing loyalty and self-interest is crucial because it affects the quality of personal and professional relationships. If one is too loyal, they may be taken advantage of or become a doormat for others. Conversely, if one is too self-interested, they may become selfish and neglectful of others' needs, which can lead to strained relationships.

Moreover, balancing loyalty and self-interest is vital for personal growth and development. Being loyal to someone or a group can often limit one's opportunities and hinder their progress. On the other hand, being too self-interested can also result in a lack of personal growth, as it can make one overly focused on achieving personal goals at the expense of developing meaningful relationships.

BALANCING LYALTY AND SELF-INTEREST

How to Balance Loyalty and Personal Goals

Balancing loyalty and personal goals involves setting boundaries and being mindful of one's actions. Here are some strategies that can be employed:

1. Reflect on Your Values: It's important to reflect on your values and what is most important to you. This will help you determine which relationships are worth being loyal to and which goals are worth pursuing.

2. Set Priorities: Once you've determined your values, it's important to set priorities. Determine which relationships are most important to you, and which personal goals are worth pursuing. This will help you allocate your time and energy more effectively.

3. Communicate: Communication is key to balancing loyalty and personal goals. Be transparent about your priorities and goals with those you are loyal to. This will help ensure that they understand where you are coming from and can support you in your pursuits.

4. Be Mindful of Your Actions: Be mindful of your actions and how they may affect others. Consider the impact that your actions may have on those you are loyal to and adjust your behavior accordingly.

Setting Boundaries in Loyalty

Setting boundaries is an essential component of balancing loyalty and personal goals. Here are some tips for setting boundaries:

BALANCING LOYALTY AND SELF-INTEREST

1. Identify Your Boundaries: Determine which areas of your life you are willing to be flexible in and which areas you are not. For example, you may be willing to make compromises in your work-life balance, but not in your personal relationships.

2. Communicate Your Boundaries: Once you've identified your boundaries, it's important to communicate them to others. This will help ensure that they understand your limitations and can respect them.

3. Stick to Your Boundaries: It's important to stick to your boundaries, even if it means saying no to others. This will help you maintain your integrity and ensure that your needs are being met.

The Benefits of Balancing Loyalty and Self-Interest

Balancing loyalty and self-interest can have numerous benefits. Here are some of them:

1. Stronger Relationships: Balancing loyalty and self-interest can help strengthen personal and professional relationships. By being loyal to others while also pursuing personal goals, you can create a sense of mutual respect and support.

2. Increased Personal Growth: Balancing loyalty and self-interest can help you achieve personal growth and development. By pursuing personal goals, you can expand your skills and knowledge, which can lead to new opportunities and experiences.

3. Enhanced Well-Being: Balancing loyalty and self-interest can help enhance well-being. By pursuing personal goals and maintaining meaningful relationships, you can create a sense of purpose and fulfillment in your life.

BALANCING LOYALTY AND SELF-INTEREST

4. Improved Decision-Making: Balancing loyalty and self-interest can help you make better decisions. By weighing the needs of others with your personal goals, you can make decisions that benefit everyone involved.

5. Reduced Stress: Balancing loyalty and self-interest can also reduce stress. By setting boundaries and prioritizing your time and energy, you can reduce the stress that comes with trying to please everyone.

Maintaining Loyalty Without Sacrificing Personal Growth

Maintaining loyalty without sacrificing personal growth is a delicate balance. Here are some strategies that can help:

1. Identify Your Values and Goals: It's important to identify your values and personal goals. This will help you determine which relationships are worth being loyal to and which personal goals are worth pursuing.

2. Communicate Your Priorities: Communicate your priorities to those you are loyal to. This will help ensure that they understand your motivations and can support you in your pursuits.

3. Be Flexible: Be flexible in your approach to loyalty. You may need to make compromises in certain situations to ensure that your personal goals are being met.

4. Be Open to Change: Be open to change and new opportunities. Loyalty doesn't necessarily mean staying in the same situation forever. Be willing to explore new paths and opportunities that align with your values and goals.

BALANCING LOYALTY AND SELF-INTEREST

Examples of Balancing Loyalty and Self-Interest in Personal and Professional Life

Here are some examples of balancing loyalty and self-interest in personal and professional life:

1. Personal Life: Sarah has been best friends with Maria since childhood. Sarah is also an aspiring artist and spends much of her free time painting. To balance her loyalty to Maria and her personal goals, Sarah communicates her priorities to Maria and sets boundaries around her time. Sarah also invites Maria to her art shows and asks for her support.

2. Professional Life: Joe is a team leader at a software company. Joe is also interested in pursuing a side business as a consultant. To balance his loyalty to his team and his personal goals, Joe communicates his priorities to his team and sets boundaries around his time. Joe also looks for opportunities to use his consulting skills to benefit his team.

3. Family Life: Lisa is a busy mother of two young children. Lisa also has a passion for running and competes in marathons. To balance her loyalty to her family and her personal goals, Lisa communicates her priorities to her family and sets boundaries around her time. Lisa also includes her family in her running activities and encourages them to support her.

Conclusion

Balancing loyalty and self-interest is a complex task that requires careful reflection and communication. By setting boundaries, prioritizing goals, and being flexible, you can maintain meaningful relationships while also achieving personal growth and development. Balancing loyalty and self-interest can lead to stronger relationships, increased personal growth, enhanced well-being, improved decision-making, and reduced stress.

**AS WE MOVE INTO
THIS NEXT CHAPTER**

CHAPTER 6
The Role of Communication in Loyalty

In business, loyalty is the currency that fosters long-lasting partnerships and sustainable success."

\#LoyaltyInEverything

CHAPTER 6
The Role of Communication in Loyalty

Introduction

Loyalty is a critical component of any successful business. Building loyalty among customers is essential to ensuring that they continue to do business with a company and remain satisfied with the products or services provided. Communication can help to establish a sense of connection between the company and its customers, create a sense of shared purpose, and foster trust and loyalty. Communication is a fundamental tool for building loyalty, and it is critical to understand its role in this process. In this chapter, we will explore the importance of communication in building loyalty, effective communication strategies for building and maintaining loyalty, the role of active listening in loyalty, building trust through open communication, the benefits of honest communication in loyalty, and examples of effective communication in building loyalty.

Loyalty is one of the key elements in the success of any business or organization. It is the foundation of any long-term relationship between a company and its customers or stakeholders. Building loyalty requires a deep understanding of the needs and desires of your customers, as well as effective communication strategies that promote trust and confidence. Effective communication is one of the most important tools for building loyalty. .

THE ROLE OF COMMUNICATION IN LOYALTY

The Importance of Communication in Building Loyalty

Communication is the foundation upon which loyalty is built. Effective communication creates a connection between a company and its customers, making them feel valued, understood, and appreciated. When customers feel that a company is listening to their needs and concerns, they are more likely to remain loyal to that company. By communicating effectively with customers, companies can demonstrate that they understand their needs and are committed to meeting them. Moreover, communication helps customers understand what a company stands for, what its values are, and how it differentiates itself from its competitors.

Effective communication can help create a positive customer experience, which is critical in building loyalty. A positive customer experience is one that meets or exceeds customers' expectations and leaves them feeling satisfied with their interaction with a company. Communication is key to delivering this positive experience by providing customers with the information they need, responding to their questions and concerns, and showing them that their feedback is valued. When customers feel valued, they are more likely to remain loyal to a company, even in the face of competition.

How to Effectively Communicate Loyalty

To effectively communicate loyalty, companies must first understand what loyalty means to their customers. Loyalty can mean different things to different people, so it's essential to understand what customers value most in a relationship with a company. This requires active listening and a willingness to engage with customers on a personal level.

THE ROLE OF COMMUNICATION IN LOYALTY

If a company wants to communicate loyalty more effectively they should focus on the following key elements:

1. Consistency: Consistency is key when it comes to building loyalty. Companies need to ensure that they are communicating their message consistently across all channels and touchpoints.

2. Clarity: Clarity is also important in effective communication. Companies need to ensure that their message is clear and easy to understand. This means avoiding jargon and using simple, straightforward language.

3. Relevance: Communication needs to be relevant to the customer. Companies need to understand their customers' needs and desires and tailor their communication accordingly.

4. Timing: Timing is also important in effective communication. Companies need to communicate with their customers at the right time, whether it's during a sale or after a customer service interaction.

Once a company has a good understanding of what loyalty means to its customers, it can begin to develop a communication strategy that effectively communicates loyalty. The strategy should include clear and concise messaging that is aligned with the company's values and mission. Communication channels should also be carefully considered, with an emphasis on those that are most likely to reach the target audience.

THE ROLE OF COMMUNICATION IN LOYALTY

The Role of Active Listening in Loyalty

Active listening is an essential component of effective communication and plays a critical role in building loyalty. Active listening involves giving your full attention to the person speaking, seeking to understand their perspective, asking questions, and providing feedback. This can be achieved through verbal and non-verbal cues, such as nodding, maintaining eye contact, and reflecting back what was said to ensure understanding. Active listening helps to create a sense of connection and trust between the company and its customers.

Active listening shows customers that their opinions and feedback are valued, which is essential in building loyalty. Active listening also helps companies to better understand their customers' needs and desires. By actively listening to customers, companies can gain valuable insights into their needs, preferences, and concerns, allowing them to tailor their products or services to better meet customer expectations.

Building Trust through Open Communication

Trust is a critical component of loyalty. Customers must trust a company to provide quality products or services, deliver on its promises, and act with integrity. Open communication is a key factor in building trust, as it allows companies to be transparent with their customers.

Open communication involves being honest and transparent with customers, even when it may be uncomfortable or difficult. This includes acknowledging mistakes and taking responsibility for them, providing accurate and timely information, and actively seeking feedback from customers. By communicating openly and honestly, companies can establish trust with their customers, which is essential in building long-term loyalty.

THE ROLE OF COMMUNICATION IN LOYALTY

By being open and transparent with customers, companies can demonstrate their commitment to building trust and fostering loyalty. This can help to create a sense of connection and shared purpose between the company and its customers.

The Benefits of Honest Communication in Loyalty

Honest communication is a critical component of building loyalty. When customers feel that a company is honest and transparent with them, they are more likely to trust that company and remain loyal to it. Honesty is also essential in addressing customer concerns and resolving issues in a timely and effective manner. This can help prevent negative experiences from turning into permanent issues that erode customer loyalty.

Honest communication can foster a culture of openness and transparency within a company. When employees are encouraged to communicate honestly with customers, they are more likely to take ownership of issues and work to resolve them quickly. This can lead to a more engaged workforce, which can have a positive impact on customer loyalty.

Honest communication also helps companies to manage customer expectations. By being upfront about what they can and cannot deliver, companies can avoid disappointing their customers and damaging their trust and loyalty. Honesty also helps to prevent misunderstandings and miscommunications, which can lead to frustration and dissatisfaction.

THE ROLE OF COMMUNICATION IN LOYALTY

Examples of Effective Communication in Building Loyalty

There are many examples of effective communication strategies that can help to build loyalty. Here are a few examples:

1. Personalization: Personalization involves tailoring communication to the specific needs and preferences of individual customers. This can involve using customer data to personalize marketing messages or using a customer's name in communication.

2. Customer feedback: Soliciting feedback from customers is an important element of effective communication. By asking for feedback, companies demonstrate that they care about their customers' opinions and are committed to improving their products and services.

3. Social media: Social media can be a powerful tool for building loyalty. Companies can use social media to engage with customers, respond to their questions and concerns, and provide valuable information and insights.

4. Email marketing: Email marketing can be an effective way to build loyalty by providing customers with relevant and timely information. Companies can use email to share news about new products or services, offer exclusive discounts, or provide helpful tips and advice.

5. Customer service: Effective customer service is essential in building loyalty. Companies need to be responsive, helpful, and empathetic when dealing with customer issues and concerns.

THE ROLE OF COMMUNICATION IN LOYALTY

Here are other examples of companies that have effectively used communication to build loyalty. One such example is Amazon, which has built its entire business around customer-centricity. Amazon is known for its easy-to-use website, fast delivery times, and excellent customer service. The company has a robust feedback system that encourages customers to leave reviews and provide feedback on their experiences. Amazon also communicates proactively with customers by providing updates on shipping and delivery times, making it easy for customers to track their orders.

Another example of effective communication in building loyalty is Apple. Apple's brand is built around innovation, design, and user experience. The company has a loyal following of customers who appreciate the quality of its products and the seamless integration between hardware and software. Apple has built its brand by communicating its values and mission through marketing and advertising campaigns that focus on simplicity and user experience.

Zappos is another example of a company that has effectively used communication to build loyalty. Zappos is an online shoe retailer that has built a reputation for exceptional customer service. The company's website is designed to be easy to use, and it offers free shipping and returns. Zappos also has a robust feedback system that encourages customers to leave reviews and provide feedback on their experiences. The company is known for its personalized service, with representatives available to assist customers 24/7 via phone or chat.

Conclusion

Communication is a critical component of building and maintaining loyalty. Effective communication can help create a positive customer experience, establish a sense of connection and shared purpose, foster trust and confidence, which is essential creating a strong foundation and building long-term relationships and loyalty. To effectively communicate and build loyalty, companies need to focus on consistency, clarity, relevance, and timing, active listening, open communication, and honesty.

Companies that prioritize communication and make it a core part of their business strategy are more likely to build strong, loyal relationships with their customers. By understanding the role of communication in loyalty and implementing effective communication strategies, companies can create a sustainable competitive advantage and achieve long-term success.

The Role of Communication in Loyalty

CHAPTER 7
The Challenges of Loyalty in Personal Relationships

"Life's journey becomes more meaningful when shared with loyal companions."

#LOYALTYINEVERYTHING

CHAPTER 7
The Challenges of Loyalty in Personal Relationships

Introduction

Loyalty is a crucial aspect of personal relationships. It can be defined as the commitment and dedication one has towards another person or group of people, particularly in times of need. Loyalty can manifest in various forms, such as staying committed to a romantic partner, being dedicated to a friend, or showing support to a family member. However, loyalty can also present several challenges in personal relationships. In this chapter, we will explore the role of loyalty in personal relationships, the challenges of loyalty in personal life, overcoming conflict through loyalty, balancing loyalty with personal growth in relationships, maintaining loyalty in the face of adversity, and the benefits of loyalty in personal relationships.

The Role of Loyalty in Personal Relationships

Loyalty is one of the essential aspects of building and maintaining personal relationships. It helps to establish trust, respect, and mutual understanding between individuals. When one person is loyal to another, it sends a message that they can be trusted and relied upon, which can help build a strong foundation for the relationship. Loyalty can also foster a sense of security and comfort, as people feel safe and supported when they know that someone is committed to them.

In romantic relationships, loyalty is essential for building a strong and lasting connection between partners. When two people commit to each other, they pledge to be loyal to each other and work towards building a life together. This loyalty helps to strengthen the bond between the partners and ensures that they can rely on each other through thick and thin.

THE CHALLENGES OF LOYALTY IN PERSONAL RELATIONSHIPS

Similarly, in friendships, loyalty plays a vital role in building a lasting connection between friends. When friends are loyal to each other, they establish a sense of trust and mutual respect that can endure over time. This loyalty helps to create a sense of camaraderie and understanding between friends, which can be invaluable in times of need.

Finally, in family relationships, loyalty is a cornerstone of building a strong and lasting connection between family members. Family members often rely on each other for support and understanding, and loyalty helps to ensure that they can count on each other in times of need.

The Challenges of Loyalty in Personal Life

While loyalty is essential in personal relationships, it can also present several challenges. One of the most significant challenges of loyalty is the conflict that can arise when one person's loyalty to another conflicts with their loyalty to themselves or to other people.

For example, in romantic relationships, loyalty can sometimes conflict with personal growth. If one partner is committed to pursuing a career or personal interest that takes them away from the relationship, the other partner may feel hurt or neglected. In such cases, loyalty can be challenging to maintain, as both partners need to balance their commitment to each other with their commitment to personal growth.

Similarly, in friendships, loyalty can sometimes conflict with personal values or other friendships. If a friend is engaging in behavior that goes against one's personal values or is hurting another friend, loyalty can be challenging to maintain. In such cases, one may need to balance their commitment to the friend with their commitment to their personal values or other friendships.

Finally, in family relationships, loyalty can sometimes conflict with one's personal desires or needs. For example, if a family member is struggling with addiction or mental health issues, their loyalty to that family member may conflict with their need to take care of their own mental health or wellbeing. In such cases, maintaining loyalty can be challenging, as family members need to balance their commitment to each other with their commitment to personal growth and wellbeing.

THE CHALLENGES OF LOYALTY IN PERSONAL RELATIONSHIPS

Overcoming Conflict Through Loyalty

While conflicts can arise due to loyalty in personal relationships, it is possible to overcome them. One of the best ways to overcome conflicts through loyalty is by fostering open and honest communication between all parties involved.

When conflicts arise, it is essential to have a candid conversation about the situation and how it is affecting each person involved. This communication can help to identify the root cause of the conflict and work towards a resolution that is satisfactory for all parties. In some cases, compromise may be necessary to balance loyalty with personal growth or other commitments.

Another way to overcome conflicts through loyalty is by setting boundaries. It is essential to establish clear boundaries about what one is willing to tolerate in a relationship and what they cannot accept. These boundaries can help to prevent conflicts from arising and ensure that loyalty is maintained while also respecting personal growth and other commitments.

Balancing Loyalty with Personal Growth in Relationships

As mentioned earlier, loyalty can sometimes conflict with personal growth in relationships. However, it is possible to balance loyalty with personal growth by establishing clear expectations and boundaries.

In romantic relationships, both partners need to understand that personal growth is essential for a healthy relationship. It is crucial to support each other in pursuing personal interests and career goals while also maintaining the commitment to the relationship. By setting clear expectations and boundaries, both partners can work towards personal growth while also maintaining their loyalty to each other.

Similarly, in friendships, it is essential to respect each other's personal growth and interests. It is crucial to support each other in pursuing personal goals while also maintaining the commitment to the friendship. By setting clear expectations and boundaries, friends can work towards personal growth while also maintaining their loyalty to each other.

THE CHALLENGES OF LOYALTY IN PERSONAL RELATIONSHIPS

Maintaining Loyalty in the Face of Adversity

Maintaining loyalty can be challenging in the face of adversity. However, it is essential to remember that loyalty is about being committed and dedicated to another person or group of people, particularly in times of need.

In personal relationships, adversity can take many forms, such as illness, financial difficulties, or emotional stress. During these times, it is crucial to stay committed to each other and support each other through the challenges.

Maintaining open and honest communication, setting clear boundaries and expectations, and being patient and understanding can help to maintain loyalty in the face of adversity.

The Benefits of Loyalty in Personal Relationships

Despite the challenges that loyalty can present in personal relationships, it is essential to remember the benefits that loyalty can bring.

Loyalty can help to establish trust and mutual respect between individuals, which can lead to strong and lasting personal relationships. Loyalty can foster a sense of security and comfort, as people feel safe and supported when they know that someone is committed to them. In romantic relationships, loyalty can help to strengthen the bond between partners and ensure that they can rely on each other through thick and thin.

In friendships, loyalty can help to create a sense of camaraderie and understanding between friends, which can be invaluable in times of need. Loyalty can help to establish a sense of trust and mutual respect that can endure over time.

THE CHALLENGES OF LOYALTY IN PERSONAL RELATIONSHIPS

Finally, in family relationships, loyalty is a cornerstone of building a strong and lasting connection between family members. Family members often rely on each other for support and understanding, and loyalty helps to ensure that they can count on each other in times of need.

Conclusion

Loyalty is a crucial aspect of personal relationships, but it can also present several challenges. Conflicts can arise when loyalty conflicts with personal growth, values, or needs. However, by fostering open and honest communication, setting clear boundaries and expectations, and being patient and understanding, conflicts can be overcome, and loyalty can be maintained. The benefits of loyalty, such as trust, mutual respect, and a sense of security, can help to build strong and lasting personal relationships.

How do you deal with the Challenges of Loyalty in your personal life?

CHAPTER 8
Overcoming Betrayal and Rebuilding Loyalty

"Loyalty is not just a virtue; it's a powerful force that can move mountains in relationships."

#LOYALTYINEVERYTHING

CHAPTER 8
Overcoming Betrayal and Rebuilding Loyalty

Introduction

Betrayal is a breach of trust or confidence that leads to a violation of a relationship. When someone we trust betrays us, it can be a deeply painful and traumatic experience. Betrayal can take many forms, from infidelity to deception, to breaking promises. Regardless of the form it takes, betrayal can undermine the very foundation of a relationship, eroding trust and loyalty.

The Role of Betrayal in Loyalty

Betrayal and loyalty are deeply interconnected. Betrayal undermines loyalty, which is built on trust, commitment, and honesty. When we feel betrayed, we may question whether we can ever trust that person again. This can lead to a breakdown in communication, increased conflict, and ultimately, the erosion of the relationship.

However, loyalty can also play a role in overcoming betrayal. When we are loyal to someone, we may be more willing to forgive them for their mistakes and work to rebuild trust. In fact, loyalty can be a key factor in rebuilding trust after betrayal.

Overcoming Betrayal and Rebuilding Trust

Overcoming betrayal and rebuilding trust requires a commitment from both parties. It can be a difficult and painful process, but with time, effort, and patience, it is possible to repair a damaged relationship.

OVERCOMING BETRAYAL AND REBUILDING LOYALTY

The first step in overcoming betrayal is acknowledging what happened. Both parties need to be honest about what happened and how it impacted the relationship. This can be a difficult conversation, but it is necessary for moving forward.

The next step is to take responsibility for one's actions. If one party betrayed the other, they need to take responsibility for their actions and acknowledge the hurt they caused. This can be a difficult and humbling process, but it is necessary for rebuilding trust.

The third step is to work on communication. Communication is key in any relationship, but it is especially important in the aftermath of betrayal. Both parties need to be open and honest about their feelings and needs. This can help to rebuild trust and create a stronger foundation for the relationship.

How to Effectively Communicate after Betrayal

Effective communication is essential in rebuilding loyalty after betrayal. The following are some tips for communicating effectively after betrayal:

1. Be honest: It is important to be honest about your feelings and needs. This can help to create a stronger foundation for the relationship.

2. Listen actively: Active listening involves paying attention to what the other person is saying and acknowledging their feelings. This can help to create a sense of empathy and understanding.

3. Avoid blame: Blaming the other person for what happened can lead to defensiveness and conflict. Instead, focus on how you can work together to move forward.

OVERCOMING BETRAYAL AND REBUILDING LOYALTY

4. Be patient: Rebuilding trust takes time, and it is important to be patient with each other. It is also important to recognize that setbacks may occur, but that doesn't mean that the relationship is doomed

Examples of Successful Rebuilding of Loyalty

There are many examples of successful rebuilding of loyalty after betrayal. One such example is the story of former U.S. President Bill Clinton and his wife, Hillary Clinton. In 1998, Bill Clinton admitted to having an extramarital affair with Monica Lewinsky, a White House intern. This revelation caused significant public backlash, and many people questioned whether the Clintons' marriage could survive.

Despite the intense scrutiny and criticism, the Clintons worked to rebuild their relationship. Hillary Clinton later wrote in her memoir that they sought counseling and that Bill Clinton apologized for his actions. They also worked to communicate more openly and honestly with each other, and they eventually were able to rebuild their relationship and their public image.

Another example of successful rebuilding of loyalty is the story of former NBA player Kobe Bryant and his wife, Vanessa Bryant. In 2003, Kobe Bryant was accused of sexually assaulting a hotel employee. The incident caused significant strain on his marriage, and Vanessa Bryant filed for divorce in 2011.

However, the couple later reconciled and worked to rebuild their relationship. Kobe Bryant publicly apologized for his actions, and the couple sought counseling to work through their issues. They also focused on communicating more effectively and being more supportive of each other. Despite the challenges they faced, they were able to rebuild their relationship and stayed married until Kobe's tragic death in 2020.

OVERCOMING BETRAYAL AND REBUILDING LOYALTY

The Benefits of Rebuilding Loyalty After Betrayal

Rebuilding loyalty after betrayal can be a difficult and painful process, but it can also have many benefits. When we work to rebuild trust and loyalty in a relationship, we can create a stronger, more resilient connection.

One of the benefits of rebuilding loyalty is that it can help to create a deeper sense of intimacy and connection. When we are able to work through difficult times together, it can help to strengthen our bond and create a greater sense of trust and loyalty.

Rebuilding loyalty can also help us to develop greater resilience and coping skills. When we are able to overcome challenges and work through difficult emotions, we can become more adept at handling stress and adversity in the future.

Another benefit of rebuilding loyalty is that it can help us to grow and learn from our mistakes. When we acknowledge our own role in a situation and work to make amends, we can develop greater self-awareness and learn from our mistakes.

Conclusion

Betrayal can be a deeply painful and traumatic experience, but it is possible to overcome it and rebuild loyalty in a relationship. This process requires a commitment from both parties to acknowledge what happened, take responsibility for one's actions, and work on communication and forgiveness.

OVERCOMING BETRAYAL AND REBUILDING LOYALTY

Rebuilding loyalty after betrayal can have many benefits, including a deeper sense of intimacy, greater resilience and coping skills, and the opportunity for personal growth and learning. While it is not always easy, it is possible to work through difficult times and create a stronger, more resilient relationship.

When you get knocked down in life, you'll find a way to somehow get back on your feet again.

CHAPTER 9
Teaching Loyalty to the Next Generation

"The strongest bridges of trust are constructed on the pillars of loyalty and integrity."

#LOYALTYINEVERYTHING

CHAPTER 9
Teaching Loyalty to the Next Generation

Introduction

Loyalty is a crucial virtue that has been valued in many cultures throughout history. It is the quality of being faithful to someone or something, and it involves a strong sense of commitment, trust, and dedication. In today's world, loyalty is more important than ever before, as we face various challenges and uncertainties in our personal and professional lives. Therefore, it is essential to teach loyalty to the next generation so that they can become responsible and trustworthy members of society.

The Importance of Teaching Loyalty to Children

Teaching loyalty to children is essential because it helps them develop a strong sense of commitment and dedication. Loyalty teaches children to stick to their promises and fulfill their obligations, even when things get tough. It helps them build meaningful relationships based on trust and respect, which are crucial for personal and professional success. Additionally, loyalty also teaches children to be responsible and dependable, which are essential qualities for leadership positions.

Children who grow up with a strong sense of loyalty are more likely to be successful in their personal and professional lives. They are more likely to form long-lasting relationships, build successful careers, and become respected members of their communities. Furthermore, they are also more likely to have a positive impact on the world around them, as they are driven by a sense of purpose and dedication.

TEACHING LOYALTY TO THE NEXT GENERATION

How to Effectively Teach Loyalty to Children

Teaching loyalty to children is not an easy task, as it requires a great deal of patience, dedication, and understanding. However, there are several effective strategies that parents, teachers, and mentors can use to teach loyalty to children. Some of these strategies include:

1. Setting a good example: Children learn by example, so it is essential for parents, teachers, and mentors to model loyalty in their own behavior. They should demonstrate their commitment to their family, friends, and work by fulfilling their obligations, sticking to their promises, and being dependable.
2. Using positive reinforcement: Positive reinforcement is a powerful tool that can be used to reinforce loyalty in children. Parents, teachers, and mentors should praise children when they exhibit loyalty, and they should also reward them for their loyalty.
3. Encouraging open communication: Loyalty is built on trust and communication, so it is important to encourage children to communicate openly and honestly with others. This can be achieved by listening actively, being non-judgmental, and showing empathy.
4. Teaching the value of loyalty: Children should be taught the value of loyalty and how it can benefit them in their personal and professional lives. They should be encouraged to view loyalty as an essential quality that is worth pursuing.

Building Loyalty through Positive Reinforcement

Positive reinforcement is one of the most effective ways to build loyalty in children. This involves rewarding children when they exhibit loyalty and demonstrating the benefits of loyalty in their lives. Positive reinforcement can take many forms, including verbal praise, physical rewards, and public recognition.

TEACHING LOYALTY TO THE NEXT GENERATION

Verbal praise is a simple but effective way to reinforce loyalty in children. When a child exhibits loyalty, parents, teachers, and mentors should praise them and acknowledge their efforts. For example, if a child stands up for a friend who is being bullied, the parent or teacher should praise them for their loyalty and explain how their actions have helped their friend.

Physical rewards can also be used to reinforce loyalty in children. For example, parents can give their child a small gift or treat when they exhibit loyalty. This can be a simple gesture, such as taking the child out for ice cream, or a more significant reward, such as buying them a new toy.

Public recognition is another powerful form of positive reinforcement. When a child exhibits loyalty, parents, teachers, and mentors should publicly recognize their efforts. This can be achieved by praising the child in front of their peers or colleagues, or by giving them a certificate or award. Public recognition not only reinforces the child's loyalty but also motivates other children to exhibit similar behavior.

Overcoming Negative Influences on Loyalty

Teaching loyalty to children can be challenging, especially when negative influences are present in their lives. Negative influences can come from a variety of sources, including peers, media, and societal norms. Therefore, it is important to identify these negative influences and take steps to overcome them.

Peer pressure is a common negative influence on loyalty in children. Children may be pressured by their peers to be disloyal to their friends or family, or to engage in risky or harmful behavior. To overcome peer pressure, children should be taught how to assert their independence

TEACHING LOYALTY TO THE NEXT GENERATION

and stand up for what they believe in. Parents, teachers, and mentors can also provide children with positive role models and encourage them to form healthy relationships with peers who exhibit loyalty.

Media is another negative influence on loyalty in children. Children are exposed to a vast amount of media content, including television, movies, video games, and social media. Many of these media portray disloyal behavior as glamorous or heroic, which can influence children's attitudes towards loyalty. To overcome negative media influences, children should be taught to critically evaluate media content and to question the messages it conveys. Parents, teachers, and mentors can also provide children with positive media content that promotes loyalty and positive values.

Societal norms can also be a negative influence on loyalty in children. Society often values individualism and self-interest over loyalty and commitment. Therefore, children may be taught to prioritize their own needs and desires over the needs of others. To overcome negative societal norms, children should be taught the value of community and the importance of working together towards common goals. Parents, teachers, and mentors can also provide children with positive role models who exhibit loyalty and commitment to others.

Examples of Successful Teaching of Loyalty

There are many examples of successful teaching of loyalty to children. One such example is the Big Brothers Big Sisters program, which pairs children with adult mentors who provide support and guidance. The program emphasizes the importance of loyalty and commitment and encourages children to develop strong relationships with their mentors. Studies have shown that children who participate in the program are more likely to exhibit positive behaviors, including loyalty, compared to children who do not participate.

TEACHING LOYALTY TO THE NEXT GENERATION

Another example of successful teaching of loyalty is the Boys and Girls Clubs of America. The organization provides children with a safe and supportive environment where they can learn and grow. The organization emphasizes the importance of loyalty, respect, and responsibility, and encourages children to develop positive relationships with their peers and mentors. Studies have shown that children who participate in the Boys and Girls Clubs of America are more likely to exhibit positive behaviors, including loyalty, compared to children who do not participate.

The Benefits of Teaching Loyalty to the Next Generation

Teaching loyalty to the next generation has many benefits, both for individuals and for society as a whole. Some of these benefits include:

1. Building stronger relationships: Loyalty helps individuals build strong and meaningful relationships based on trust and respect. This is essential for personal and professional success, as well as for maintaining a healthy and happy life.

2. Fostering a sense of community: Loyalty promotes a sense of community and encourages individuals to work together towards common goals. This is essential for building strong and resilient communities that can withstand challenges and uncertainties.

3. Developing responsible and dependable individuals: Loyalty teaches individuals to be responsible and dependable, which are essential qualities for success in any endeavor.

4. Promoting positive values: Loyalty promotes positive values, including commitment, dedication, and trust. These values are essential for building a better world and creating a more just and equitable society.

TEACHING LOYALTY TO THE NEXT GENERATION

Conclusion

Teaching loyalty to the next generation is essential for building stronger relationships, fostering a sense of community, developing responsible and dependable individuals, and promoting positive values. Parents, teachers, and mentors can effectively teach loyalty by modeling loyal behavior, using positive reinforcement, and overcoming negative influences. Examples of successful teaching of loyalty include programs like Big Brothers Big Sisters and Boys and Girls Clubs of America. By teaching loyalty to the next generation, we can create a better world and ensure a brighter future for generations to come.

CHAPTER 10
Loyalty in the Digital Age

"In the face of challenges, loyalty acts as a shield that protects relationships from harm."

#LOYALTYINEVERYTHING

CHAPTER 10
Loyalty in the Digital Age

Introduction

The digital age has revolutionized the way businesses operate, communicate, and connect with customers. The advent of social media and other digital platforms has enabled businesses to reach their target audiences more effectively and efficiently. However, the digital age has also presented new challenges for businesses, especially when it comes to building and maintaining loyalty.

Chapter 10 of this book explores the challenges of loyalty in the digital age and offers effective strategies for cultivating and maintaining digital loyalty. This chapter also discusses the role of technology in building loyalty, the potential risks and benefits of online loyalty, and the importance of authenticity and transparency in digital loyalty. This chapter concludes by providing examples of successful digital loyalty in personal and professional life and discussing the future of loyalty in the digital age.

The Challenges of Loyalty in the Digital Age

The digital age has presented new challenges for businesses when it comes to building and maintaining loyalty. One of the biggest challenges is the high level of competition that exists in the online space. With so many businesses vying for attention and customers online, it can be difficult for businesses to stand out and build long-term relationships with customers.

LOYALTY IN THE DIGITAL AGE

Another challenge is the changing expectations of customers in the digital age. With access to more information and choices than ever before, customers have become more demanding and expect more from the businesses they interact with. This means that businesses need to be more responsive, personalized, and engaging to build and maintain loyalty.

Building Loyalty Through Social Media and Online Communication

Social media and online communication have become essential tools for businesses looking to build and maintain loyalty in the digital age. These platforms enable businesses to connect with customers on a more personal level and build relationships that go beyond traditional transactions.

One effective strategy for building loyalty through social media is to create engaging and shareable content. This can include informative blog posts, entertaining videos, and inspiring images that resonate with your target audience. By creating content that is valuable and relevant to your customers, you can build trust and establish your brand as an authority in your industry.

Another effective strategy is to provide personalized and responsive customer service through social media. Customers expect businesses to be available and responsive on social media, and failing to meet these expectations can result in lost loyalty. By providing quick and helpful responses to customer inquiries and complaints on social media, businesses can demonstrate their commitment to customer satisfaction and build stronger relationships with customers.

LOYALTY IN THE DIGITAL AGE

The Role of Technology in Building Loyalty

Technology has played a significant role in building loyalty in the digital age. From data analytics and artificial intelligence to chatbots and virtual assistants, businesses have access to a wide range of tools and technologies that can help them build and maintain loyalty.

One of the most powerful tools for building loyalty is data analytics. By collecting and analyzing data on customer behavior, preferences, and needs, businesses can gain insights that can help them personalize their marketing and communication efforts, improve their products and services, and build stronger relationships with customers.

Another technology that has become increasingly popular for building loyalty is chatbots and virtual assistants. These tools enable businesses to provide instant and personalized customer support, 24/7, without the need for human intervention. By leveraging chatbots and virtual assistants, businesses can improve customer satisfaction, reduce response times, and build stronger relationships with customers.

Maintaining Loyalty in a Digital World

Maintaining loyalty in a digital world requires a different approach than traditional loyalty-building strategies. In addition to providing excellent products and services, businesses need to focus on building relationships with customers and providing personalized experiences that meet their evolving needs and expectations.

LOYALTY IN THE DIGITAL AGE

One effective strategy for maintaining loyalty in a digital world is to stay engaged with customers through regular communication. This can include sending personalized emails, offering exclusive promotions and discounts, and providing updates on new products and services. By staying top of mind with customers, businesses can reinforce their commitment to customer satisfaction and build stronger relationships over time.

Another effective strategy is to offer loyalty programs that provide customers with rewards and incentives for their continued patronage. Loyalty programs can include points-based systems, exclusive discounts and promotions, and VIP treatment, among others. By offering valuable rewards and benefits, businesses can incentivize customers to remain loyal and continue to engage with their brand.

The Potential Risks and Benefits of Online Loyalty

While online loyalty can bring many benefits for businesses, it also presents potential risks. One of the biggest risks is the potential for negative reviews and feedback to spread quickly on social media and other digital platforms. A single negative review or complaint can quickly escalate and damage a business's reputation, potentially resulting in lost customers and revenue.

On the other hand, online loyalty also presents many benefits for businesses. For example, online loyalty can enable businesses to reach a wider audience, build stronger relationships with customers, and increase customer satisfaction and retention. By leveraging the power of social media and other digital platforms, businesses can engage with customers in new and innovative ways, and build a loyal customer base that can drive long-term growth and success.

Effective Strategies for Cultivating and Maintaining Digital Loyalty

There are several effective strategies that businesses can use to cultivate and maintain digital loyalty. One such strategy is to focus on providing excellent customer service at every touchpoint. This means being responsive, helpful, and empathetic, and providing personalized solutions to customer problems and complaints.

Another effective strategy is to leverage the power of social proof and user-generated content. By showcasing positive customer reviews, testimonials, and social media posts, businesses can demonstrate their value and build trust with potential customers. User-generated content, such as customer photos and videos, can also help to humanize a brand and build stronger relationships with customers.

The Importance of Authenticity and Transparency in Digital Loyalty

Authenticity and transparency are crucial components of digital loyalty. Customers today expect businesses to be honest, transparent, and authentic in their communication and branding efforts. Businesses that fail to meet these expectations risk damaging their reputation and losing the trust of their customers.

To build authentic and transparent relationships with customers, businesses should focus on being genuine and honest in all their communication and branding efforts. This means being open and transparent about their products and services, as well as their business practices and values. Businesses should also be responsive and transparent in their customer interactions, addressing any concerns or complaints promptly and honestly.

LOYALTY IN THE DIGITAL AGE

Examples of Successful Digital Loyalty in Personal and Professional Life

There are many examples of successful digital loyalty in both personal and professional life. For example, social media influencers who have built large and loyal followings have been able to monetize their influence and build successful businesses around their personal brands. Similarly, many businesses have been able to build loyal customer bases through social media and other digital platforms, by providing excellent customer service and personalized experiences.

Another example of successful digital loyalty is the growth of subscription-based services. Subscription services such as Netflix, Spotify, and Amazon Prime have built large and loyal customer bases by providing personalized and convenient experiences that meet the evolving needs and expectations of their customers.

The Future of Loyalty in the Digital Age

The future of loyalty in the digital age is likely to be characterized by increased personalization, convenience, and engagement. As technology continues to evolve, businesses will have access to even more tools and data that can help them build stronger relationships with customers and provide more personalized experiences.

One trend that is likely to continue is the growth of subscription-based services. As customers become more accustomed to the convenience and personalized experiences offered by subscription services, businesses in a wide range of industries are likely to adopt this model to build loyal customer bases and drive long-term growth.

LOYALTY IN THE DIGITAL AGE

Another trend that is likely to continue is the increasing use of artificial intelligence and machine learning to provide personalized recommendations and experiences to customers. By leveraging data and advanced algorithms, businesses can offer tailored product recommendations, personalized marketing campaigns, and targeted loyalty programs that cater to the specific needs and preferences of each customer.

Virtual and augmented reality are also likely to play a growing role in building digital loyalty in the future. By providing immersive and interactive experiences, businesses can create more engaging and memorable interactions with customers, and build stronger emotional connections with their brand.

Finally, the increasing importance of social and environmental responsibility is likely to shape the future of digital loyalty. Customers today are increasingly conscious of the impact that businesses have on society and the environment, and are looking for brands that share their values and prioritize sustainability. Businesses that are able to demonstrate their commitment to social and environmental responsibility are likely to build more loyal and engaged customer bases in the future.

Conclusion

Loyalty in the digital age presents many challenges and opportunities for businesses. While the digital landscape offers new and innovative ways to engage with customers and build loyal customer bases, it also presents potential risks and challenges that businesses must navigate carefully.

LOYALTY IN THE DIGITAL AGE

To succeed in building digital loyalty, businesses must focus on providing excellent customer service, leveraging the power of social proof and user-generated content, and being authentic and transparent in their communication and branding efforts. By adopting these strategies, businesses can build stronger relationships with customers, increase customer satisfaction and retention, and drive long-term growth and success in the digital age.

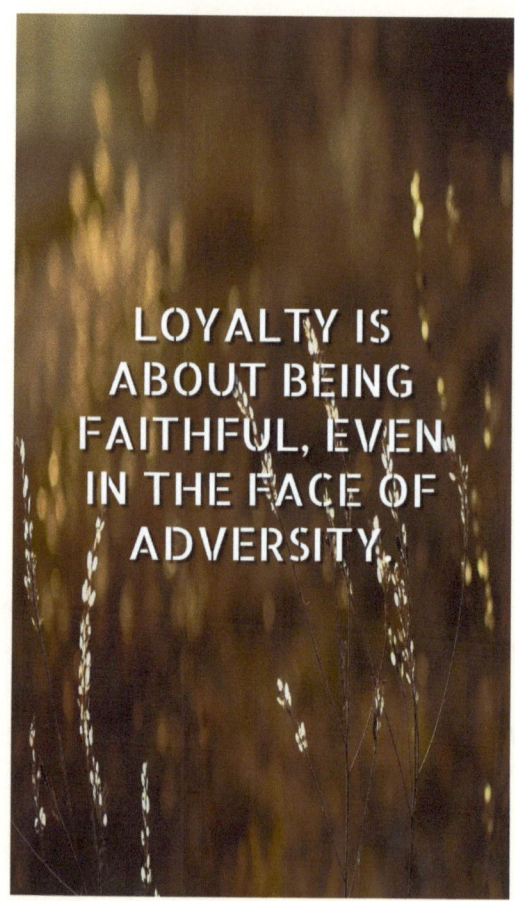

CHAPTER 11
The Dark Side of Loyalty

"A LOYAL TEAM IS A FORCE TO BE RECKONED WITH, CAPABLE OF ACHIEVING GREATNESS TOGETHER."

#LOYALTYINEVERYTHING

CHAPTER 11
The Dark Side of Loyalty

Introduction

Loyalty is often seen as a positive trait that reflects our commitment, dedication, and support towards people, organizations, and ideas that matter to us. Whether it's loyalty towards our family, friends, partners, or employers, we tend to view it as a badge of honor that defines our character and integrity. However, like any other virtue, loyalty has its limitations, and its dark side can have severe consequences for ourselves and others.

The Potential Dangers of Blind Loyalty

One of the main risks of loyalty is that it can become blind and uncritical, leading us to overlook or justify harmful behaviors or actions of those we are loyal to. This blind loyalty can stem from several factors, such as fear of abandonment, desire for acceptance and approval, or a belief that loyalty is an absolute and unconditional virtue.

Blind loyalty can result in several negative outcomes, such as enabling toxic or abusive behaviors, perpetuating injustice and inequality, or undermining our own well-being and values. For instance, someone who is blindly loyal to a family member who is a substance abuser may continue to provide financial and emotional support despite the harm it causes to both parties.

The Potential Dangers of Blind Loyalty

One of the main risks of loyalty is that it can become blind and uncritical, leading us to overlook or justify harmful behaviors or actions of those we are loyal to. This blind loyalty can stem from several factors, such as fear of abandonment, desire for acceptance and approval, or a belief

THE DARK SIDE OF LOYALTY

that loyalty is an absolute and unconditional virtue.

Blind loyalty can result in several negative outcomes, such as enabling toxic or abusive behaviors, perpetuating injustice and inequality, or undermining our own well-being and values. For instance, someone who is blindly loyal to a family member who is a substance abuser may continue to provide financial and emotional support despite the harm it causes to both parties.

Understanding the limitations of loyalty

To avoid the dangers of blind loyalty, it's essential to understand its limitations and boundaries. Loyalty should never be a justification for violating ethical or legal standards, compromising our own values and beliefs, or tolerating harmful behaviors from others.

Moreover, loyalty is not an absolute virtue, and its extent and scope should be based on rational and critical assessment rather than blind adherence. We should ask ourselves whether our loyalty is serving a constructive purpose, whether it aligns with our values and beliefs, and whether it's mutual and reciprocal.

The Risks of Loyalty in Toxic or Abusive Relationships

One of the most challenging scenarios where loyalty can be damaging is in toxic or abusive relationships, where loyalty can become a tool of manipulation and control. In such situations, the abuser often uses loyalty to keep the victim trapped in the relationship, making them feel guilty, ashamed, or afraid of leaving.

Loyalty can also become a mechanism of self-denial, where the victim downplays or ignores the severity of the abuse, rationalizes the abuser's behavior, or blames themselves for the abuse. This self-denial can prevent the victim from seeking help, healing, or justice, prolonging their suffering and trauma.

THE DARK SIDE OF LOYALTY

How to recognize and address loyalty that is damaging to yourself or others

Recognizing and addressing loyalty that is damaging to ourselves or others requires courage, honesty, and self-awareness. Here are some steps that can help:

1. Reflect on your loyalty: Take a moment to examine the reasons behind your loyalty and the extent to which it's serving a constructive purpose. Ask yourself whether your loyalty is based on mutual respect and trust, whether it's consistent with your values and beliefs, and whether it's helping or harming yourself and others.

2. Identify red flags: Be aware of the warning signs that indicate that your loyalty is becoming toxic or abusive. These may include feeling trapped or manipulated, experiencing emotional or physical harm, or witnessing harmful behaviors towards others.

3. Seek support: Don't hesitate to seek help and support from trusted friends, family, or professionals if you feel that your loyalty is becoming harmful. They can provide you with perspective, guidance, and resources to address the situation.

4. Set boundaries: Setting healthy boundaries is crucial in preventing loyalty from becoming toxic or abusive. It means defining your limits, communicating them clearly, and enforcing them consistently. It also means respecting the boundaries of others and not crossing them without their consent.

THE DARK SIDE OF LOYALTY

The importance of setting healthy boundaries in loyalty

Setting healthy boundaries is essential in cultivating healthy and constructive loyalty. It allows us to balance our loyalty with our autonomy, self-respect, and well-being, and to avoid becoming enmeshed or codependent with those we are loyal to.

Healthy boundaries also allow us to hold others accountable for their actions, to communicate our needs and expectations clearly, and to assert our rights and dignity. They create a framework for respectful and mutually beneficial relationships, where loyalty is based on trust, respect, and reciprocity.

Examples of overcoming the dark side of loyalty in personal and professional life

Overcoming the dark side of loyalty requires awareness, courage, and resilience, as well as a willingness to challenge our assumptions, beliefs, and behaviors. Here are some examples of how individuals have addressed loyalty that was damaging in their personal and professional lives:

1. Speaking out against injustice: Many individuals who have experienced or witnessed injustice and discrimination have challenged the loyalty to their organizations or communities that perpetuate these issues. For example, whistleblowers who expose corruption or wrongdoing in their companies or governments often face backlash and retaliation, but they also contribute to creating a more ethical and accountable culture.

2. Ending toxic relationships: Ending toxic or abusive relationships requires breaking free from the grip of loyalty that can keep us trapped in harmful dynamics. For example, survivors of domestic violence or

THE DARK SIDE OF LOYALTY

abuse often need to overcome the guilt, shame, and fear that come with leaving their abusers and seek support and resources to heal and rebuild their lives.

3. Setting boundaries in the workplace: Setting boundaries in the workplace can help individuals avoid burnout, harassment, and exploitation. For example, employees who assert their rights to fair treatment, reasonable workload, and respectful communication with their bosses and colleagues can create a healthier and more productive work environment.

4. Resisting peer pressure: Resisting peer pressure can help individuals stay true to their values and beliefs, even when they go against the norm or the group's loyalty. For example, teenagers who choose not to engage in risky or harmful behaviors such as drug use or bullying can inspire others to do the same and create a positive peer culture.

Conclusion

Loyalty is a complex and multifaceted virtue that can bring both benefits and risks to our lives. While loyalty can inspire us to commit ourselves to people, causes, and ideas that matter, it can also lead us to overlook or justify harmful behaviors or become trapped in toxic or abusive relationships. Recognizing and addressing the dark side of loyalty requires critical thinking, self-awareness, and courage, as well as a willingness to set healthy boundaries, hold others accountable, and speak out against injustice. Ultimately, healthy and constructive loyalty is based on trust, respect, and reciprocity, where the well-being and dignity of all parties are prioritized.

As we move from the Dark side of Loyalty into the next chapter

CHAPTER 12
Loyalty as a Two-Way Street

"Loyalty is like a tapestry, weaving threads of trust and respect into the fabric of every connection."

#LOYALTYINEVERYTHING

CHAPTER 12
Loyalty as a Two-Way Street

Introduction

Loyalty is a vital component in any relationship, be it personal or professional. It is an important aspect of trust and plays a crucial role in building lasting and meaningful connections with people. However, loyalty cannot be a one-sided affair. It is a two-way street, and both parties involved need to be loyal to each other for a relationship to thrive. This chapter will explore the importance of reciprocity in loyalty, the dangers of one-sided loyalty, how to cultivate mutual loyalty in personal and professional relationships, the benefits of reciprocal loyalty in achieving success, the role of compromise in maintaining mutual loyalty, and provide examples of successful two-way loyalty in personal and professional life.

The Importance of Reciprocity in Loyalty

Reciprocity is the foundation of mutual loyalty. It is the idea that if someone does something for you, you should do something for them in return. It is a give-and-take dynamic that is essential for any relationship to flourish. In the context of loyalty, reciprocity means that if someone is loyal to you, you should be loyal to them as well.

Reciprocity is essential because it helps to establish trust between two parties. When someone is loyal to you, it means that they have your best interests at heart. They are willing to go above and beyond to support you, and they expect the same level of commitment from you. This mutual trust creates a sense of security in the relationship, and both parties can rely on each other to be there when needed.You

THE IMPORTANCE OF RECIPROCITY IN LOYALTY

The Dangers of One-Sided Loyalty

One-sided loyalty can be dangerous and lead to negative consequences in a relationship. When one party is loyal, and the other is not, it creates an imbalance in the relationship. The loyal party can feel taken advantage of or unappreciated, while the other party can become complacent and take the loyalty for granted. This can lead to resentment and ultimately, the breakdown of the relationship.

One-sided loyalty can also be a sign of an unhealthy relationship dynamic. It can indicate that one party is more invested in the relationship than the other. This can be particularly damaging in a professional context, where one party may be exploiting the other for their own gain.

How to Cultivate Mutual Loyalty in Personal and Professional Relationships

Cultivating mutual loyalty requires effort from both parties involved. Here are some ways to foster a two-way street of loyalty:

1. Communicate: Open and honest communication is the foundation of any healthy relationship. Both parties should communicate their needs and expectations, as well as any concerns they may have. This will help to establish trust and ensure that both parties are on the same page.

2. Show appreciation: It is important to show appreciation for the loyalty of the other party. This can be as simple as saying thank you or acknowledging their efforts. When someone feels appreciated, they are more likely to continue being loyal.

3. Be reliable: Reliability is a key component of loyalty. Both parties should be dependable and follow through on their commitments. This

THE IMPORTANCE OF RECIPROCITY IN LOYALTY

will build trust and establish a sense of security in the relationship.

4. Be supportive: Supporting each other through both good times and bad is essential for cultivating mutual loyalty. This means being there for each other emotionally, mentally, and physically.

The Benefits of Reciprocal Loyalty in Achieving Success

Reciprocal loyalty can have numerous benefits, particularly in a professional context. When both parties are loyal to each other, they can work together to achieve success. Here are some of the benefits of reciprocal loyalty:

1. Increased productivity: When both parties are loyal to each other, they are more likely to work together efficiently and effectively. This can lead to increased productivity and better results.

2. Improved communication: Reciprocal loyalty requires open and honest communication. When both parties are committed to the relationship, they are more likely to communicate effectively, which can lead to a better understanding of each other's needs, expectations, and goals.

3. Stronger team dynamic: In a professional setting, reciprocal loyalty can create a stronger team dynamic. When team members are loyal to each other, they are more likely to work collaboratively and support each other, leading to a more cohesive and successful team.

4. Increased job satisfaction: Reciprocal loyalty can also lead to increased job satisfaction. When employees feel that their loyalty is reciprocated, they are more likely to feel valued and appreciated, leading to a greater sense of job satisfaction.

THE IMPORTANCE OF RECIPROCITY IN LOYALTY

The Role of Compromise in Maintaining Mutual Loyalty

Compromise is an essential component of maintaining mutual loyalty. It requires both parties to be willing to make concessions for the benefit of the relationship. When both parties are committed to compromise, they can work together to find solutions that meet both their needs.

Compromise also helps to prevent the relationship from becoming one-sided. When both parties are willing to make compromises, it shows that they are equally invested in the relationship, and they are committed to finding solutions that work for both parties.

Examples of Successful Two-Way Loyalty in Personal and Professional Life

There are many examples of successful two-way loyalty in both personal and professional life. Here are a few examples:

1. Oprah Winfrey and Gayle King: Oprah Winfrey and Gayle King have been best friends for over 40 years. Their loyalty to each other is evident in the way they support each other personally and professionally. They have both spoken publicly about their friendship and how they have supported each other through difficult times.

2. Steve Jobs and Tim Cook: Steve Jobs and Tim Cook had a strong working relationship that was built on mutual loyalty. When Steve Jobs became ill, he chose Tim Cook to succeed him as CEO of Apple. This decision was a testament to the trust and loyalty Jobs had in Cook.

3. Joe Biden and Barack Obama: Joe Biden and Barack Obama had a strong personal and professional relationship that was built on mutual loyalty. Obama chose Biden as his Vice President because he trusted him

THE IMPORTANCE OF RECIPROCITY IN LOYALTY

and valued his experience and expertise. Biden has also spoken publicly about his loyalty to Obama, and how he continues to support him even after leaving office.

Conclusion

In conclusion, loyalty is a vital component in any relationship, but it cannot be a one-sided affair. Reciprocity is essential for building trust and creating a sense of security in the relationship. Cultivating mutual loyalty requires effort from both parties, including open communication, appreciation, reliability, and support. The benefits of reciprocal loyalty can be seen in both personal and professional life, including increased productivity, improved communication, a stronger team dynamic, and increased job satisfaction. Finally, compromise is essential for maintaining mutual loyalty and preventing the relationship from becoming one-sided.

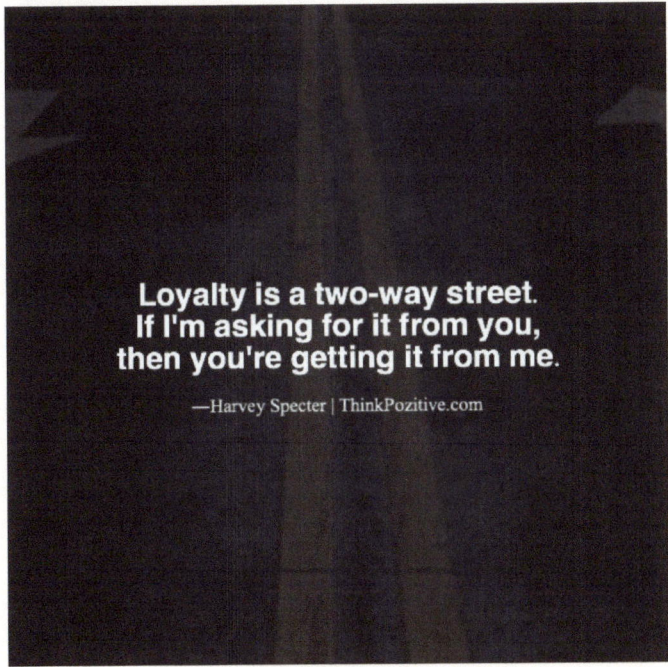

AS WE WALK THROUGH THIS JOURNEY OF LOYALTY IN EVERYTHING LETS HELP OUR BROTHER

CHAPTER 13
Balancing Loyalty and Diversity

"ONE LOYAL FRIEND IS WORTH MORE THAN A HUNDRED FAIR-WEATHER ACQUAINTANCES."

#LOYALTYINEVERYTHING

CHAPTER 13
Balancing Loyalty and Diversity

Introduction

Loyalty and diversity are two critical components of personal and professional relationships. While loyalty is essential for building trust and commitment in relationships, diversity is essential for fostering growth, creativity, and innovation. However, balancing loyalty and diversity can be challenging, especially when conflicts arise between different groups or individuals. In this chapter, we will discuss the challenges of balancing loyalty and diversity, how to maintain loyalty while respecting diversity, the importance of inclusive loyalty in personal and professional relationships, examples of successfully navigating loyalty in diverse environments, the benefits of diversity in loyalty, and the potential risks of ignoring diversity in loyalty.

The Challenges of Balancing Loyalty and Diversity

One of the significant challenges of balancing loyalty and diversity is that loyalty can sometimes conflict with diversity. For example, suppose an individual is loyal to a particular group or community that has a history of discrimination or bias towards other groups. In that case, their loyalty can be perceived as a threat to diversity and inclusion. Moreover, when loyalty is based on personal preferences, cultural or religious beliefs, it can clash with the diversity of others who have different values and beliefs.

Another challenge of balancing loyalty and diversity is that it requires individuals to be open-minded and willing to accept different perspectives, ideas, and values. However, many people struggle with embracing diversity because of their biases and prejudices. They may

BALANCING LOYALTY AND DIVERSITY

feel threatened by people who are different from them and resist change, even when it is necessary for growth and progress embracing diversity because of their biases and prejudices. They may feel threatened by people who are different from them and resist change, even when it is necessary for growth and progress.

How to maintain loyalty while respecting diversity

Maintaining loyalty while respecting diversity requires individuals to strike a delicate balance between the two. One way to do this is by being inclusive and empathetic towards others. This means being mindful of other people's needs, perspectives, and experiences, and acknowledging and valuing them. When individuals are inclusive, they can build strong relationships with people from diverse backgrounds while maintaining their loyalty to their own group or community.

Another way to maintain loyalty while respecting diversity is to communicate effectively. When conflicts arise, individuals should be willing to listen to different viewpoints and try to understand where others are coming from. They should avoid making assumptions or jumping to conclusions and instead focus on finding common ground and solutions that work for everyone.

The importance of inclusive loyalty in personal and professional relationships

Inclusive loyalty is crucial in personal and professional relationships because it promotes trust, respect, and mutual understanding. When individuals are loyal to their friends, family, colleagues, or clients, they build strong bonds that can withstand challenges and conflicts. Moreover, when they are inclusive, they create a sense of belonging and community that fosters growth, creativity, and innovation.

Inclusive loyalty also contributes to a positive work culture that

BALANCING LOYALTY AND DIVERSITY

encourages collaboration, open communication, and mutual respect. When individuals feel valued and supported, they are more likely to be engaged, productive, and committed to their work. This, in turn, can lead to higher job satisfaction, better performance, and lower turnover rates.

Examples of Successfully Navigating Loyalty in Diverse Environments

There are many examples of individuals and organizations that have successfully navigated loyalty in diverse environments. One such example is Patagonia, a clothing company that is committed to sustainability and social responsibility. Patagonia has built a loyal customer base by promoting its values and mission, which resonate with people who care about the environment and social justice. At the same time, Patagonia has embraced diversity by promoting inclusivity and diversity in its hiring practices and supplier relationships.

Another example is the United States Military, which has a diverse and inclusive culture that values loyalty, respect, and professionalism. Despite the challenges of serving in a complex and often dangerous environment, military personnel are committed to upholding their values and protecting their fellow service members. This loyalty is evident in the strong bonds that develop between military personnel, regardless of their background, ethnicity, or gender. The military has also made efforts to embrace diversity by promoting equal opportunity, providing cultural sensitivity training, and recognizing the contributions of minority groups.

The Benefits of Diversity in Loyalty

Diversity can bring many benefits to loyalty. When individuals are loyal to a diverse group or community, they can learn from different perspectives, experiences, and cultures. This can lead to personal.

BALANCING LOYALTY AND DIVERSITY

growth, greater empathy, and a broader understanding of the world. Moreover, when individuals are loyal to a diverse team or organization, they can tap into a wider range of talents, skills, and ideas, leading to better problem-solving and innovation

Diversity in loyalty also promotes social cohesion and reduces social divisions. When individuals are loyal to a diverse group or community, they can build bridges between different groups, promoting understanding, respect, and cooperation. This can lead to a more cohesive and harmonious society that is better equipped to tackle social and political challenges.

The Potential Risks of Ignoring Diversity in Loyalty

Ignoring diversity in loyalty can have significant consequences. When individuals are loyal only to their own group or community, they can become insular and resistant to change. This can lead to exclusion, discrimination, and conflict with other groups. Moreover, when organizations or institutions ignore diversity in their loyalty practices, they risk losing talented employees, customers, or clients who feel marginalized or undervalued.

Ignoring diversity in loyalty can also lead to a lack of innovation and progress. When individuals or organizations are not exposed to diverse perspectives, ideas, and experiences, they can become stagnant and complacent. This can lead to missed opportunities and a lack of creativity and growth.

BALANCING LOYALTY AND DIVERSITY

Conclusion

Balancing loyalty and diversity is essential for personal and professional relationships and for creating a more inclusive and equitable society. While there are challenges to achieving this balance, it is possible to maintain loyalty while respecting diversity. By being inclusive, empathetic, and open-minded, individuals and organizations can build strong relationships that promote trust, respect, and understanding. Moreover, by embracing diversity, they can tap into a wider range of talents, skills, and ideas, leading to better problem-solving and innovation. Ultimately, the benefits of balancing loyalty and diversity outweigh the risks, and it is up to each individual and organization to take responsibility for creating a more inclusive and equitable world.

CHAPTER 14
The Future of Loyalty

"Businesses thrive when they cultivate a culture of loyalty and appreciation among employees."

#LOYALTYINEVERYTHING

CHAPTER 14
The Future of Loyalty

Introduction

Loyalty has always been a crucial aspect of human relationships. In business, loyalty is the foundation of customer relationships. It helps businesses to retain customers and ensure repeat business, which is essential for growth and profitability. However, the nature of loyalty is changing rapidly in the modern world. In this chapter, we will explore the evolving nature of loyalty, the impact of technology and globalization on loyalty, how to stay ahead of the curve in loyalty, the potential benefits and challenges of future loyalty trends, the role of innovation in loyalty, and examples of successful adaptation to changing loyalty dynamics.

The Evolving Nature of Loyalty in the Modern World

The traditional view of loyalty is that it is a long-term commitment between two parties. In business, loyalty is often seen as a one-way street, with customers being loyal to a brand or company. However, this view is rapidly changing in the modern world. The rise of social media and online reviews has made it easier for customers to voice their opinions and share their experiences with others. As a result, customers are now more empowered than ever before, and they are demanding more from the businesses they engage with.

Today's customers want more than just quality products or services. They want personalized experiences that meet their specific needs and preferences. They also want to feel valued and appreciated by the businesses they engage with. This means that loyalty is no longer just about repeat business; it is about building relationships that are based on trust, respect, and mutual benefit.

THE FUTURE OF LOYALTY

The Impact of Technology and Globalization on Loyalty

Technology and globalization have had a significant impact on loyalty. Technology has made it easier for businesses to connect with customers and personalize their experiences. For example, businesses can now use data analytics to understand customer preferences and behavior, which allows them to tailor their marketing and communication strategies accordingly. Similarly, businesses can use social media platforms to engage with customers and respond to their feedback in real-time.

Globalization has also had a significant impact on loyalty. As businesses expand their operations across borders, they are exposed to new cultures, languages, and customer expectations. This means that businesses need to be more flexible and adaptable in their approach to loyalty. They need to understand the unique needs and preferences of customers in different regions and tailor their strategies accordingly.

How to Stay Ahead of the Curve in Loyalty

To stay ahead of the curve in loyalty, businesses need to be proactive in their approach. This means that they need to anticipate the changing needs and preferences of customers and adapt their strategies accordingly. Here are some tips for staying ahead of the curve in loyalty:

1. Use data analytics to understand customer behavior and preferences

2. Embrace technology to personalize customer experiences

3. Respond to customer feedback in real-time

4. Anticipate the changing needs and preferences of customers

5. Be flexible and adaptable in your approach to loyalty

THE FUTURE OF LOYALTY

The Potential Benefits and Challenges of Future Loyalty Trends

The future of loyalty is likely to be shaped by emerging trends such as artificial intelligence, blockchain, and the Internet of Things. These trends have the potential to revolutionize the way businesses engage with customers and build relationships. Here are some potential benefits and challenges of these trends:

Artificial intelligence:

Benefits: Personalized experiences, predictive analytics, and automated customer service

Challenges: Privacy concerns, lack of human touch, and ethical considerations

Blockchain:

Benefits: Enhanced security and transparency, faster transactions, and reduced costs

Challenges: Complexity, regulatory challenges, and lack of adoption

Internet of Things:

Benefits: Connected devices that provide personalized experiences, improved customer service, and real-time feedback

Challenges: Privacy concerns, security risks, and lack of standardization

THE FUTURE OF LOYALTY

The Role of Innovation in Loyalty

Innovation is crucial for businesses that want to stay ahead of the curve in loyalty. Innovation can help businesses to create new and unique experiences for their customers, differentiate themselves from competitors, and build deeper relationships with customers. Here are some examples of how innovation can be used to enhance loyalty:

1. Personalization: Businesses can use data analytics and artificial intelligence to personalize customer experiences. This could include personalized product recommendations, customized marketing messages, and tailored offers.

2. Loyalty programs: Traditional loyalty programs are no longer enough to retain customers. Businesses need to innovate and create unique loyalty programs that offer real value to customers. This could include gamification, experiential rewards, and surprise and delight offers.

3. Omnichannel experiences: Customers expect seamless experiences across all channels, including online, mobile, and in-store. Businesses need to innovate and create omnichannel experiences that provide a consistent and cohesive experience across all touchpoints.

4. Social media: Social media has become a powerful tool for businesses to engage with customers and build relationships. Innovative businesses are using social media to create unique experiences, such as social shopping, live-streamed events, and influencer marketing.

THE FUTURE OF LOYALTY

Examples of Successful Adaptation to Changing Loyalty Dynamics

Many businesses have successfully adapted to the changing nature of loyalty. Here are some examples of businesses that have successfully adapted to changing loyalty dynamics:

1. Amazon: Amazon is a prime example of a business that has embraced technology to personalize customer experiences. Amazon uses data analytics to make personalized product recommendations to customers, and it also offers a range of loyalty programs, such as Amazon Prime and Amazon Rewards Visa.

2. Starbucks: Starbucks has created a unique loyalty program that offers rewards to customers for purchases made using the Starbucks mobile app. The program also offers personalized offers and surprise and delight rewards, such as free drinks on customers' birthdays.

3. Nike: Nike has created a loyalty program called NikePlus, which offers personalized product recommendations, exclusive access to events and products, and personalized training programs.

4. Sephora: Sephora has created a unique loyalty program called Beauty Insider, which offers a range of benefits to customers, including free samples, exclusive offers, and early access to new products.

THE FUTURE OF LOYALTY

Conclusion

Loyalty is a crucial aspect of business relationships, but its nature is changing rapidly in the modern world. Businesses need to be proactive in their approach to loyalty and adapt their strategies to meet the changing needs and preferences of customers. This requires businesses to embrace technology, be flexible and adaptable, and innovate to create unique experiences that build deeper relationships with customers. By doing so, businesses can stay ahead of the curve in loyalty and ensure long-term growth and profitability.

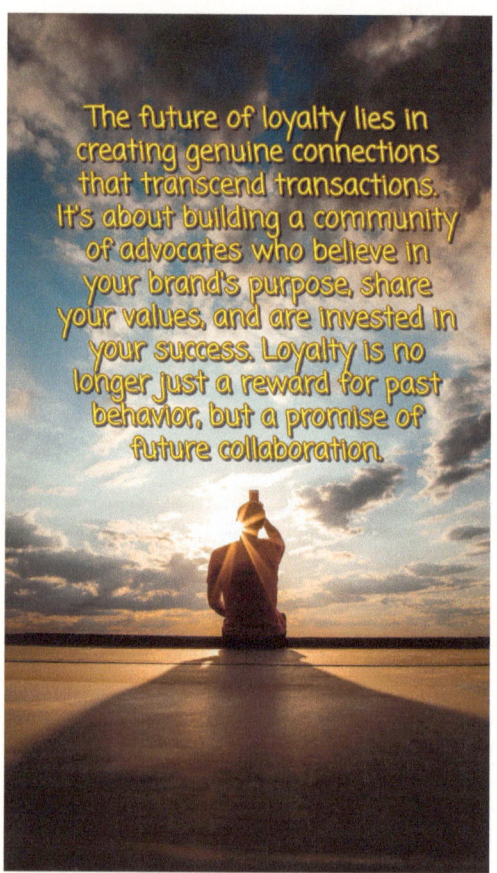

The future of loyalty lies in creating genuine connections that transcend transactions. It's about building a community of advocates who believe in your brand's purpose, share your values, and are invested in your success. Loyalty is no longer just a reward for past behavior, but a promise of future collaboration.

CHAPTER 15
Loyalty in Crisis

"Loyalty is the fuel that keeps the engine of commitment running smoothly in any partnership."

#LOYALTYINEVERYTHING

CHAPTER 15
Loyalty in Crisis

Introduction

In times of crisis, loyalty is a crucial element that can make or break an individual or organization. Loyalty is defined as a strong feeling of support or allegiance to someone or something. In the face of adversity, it is loyalty that provides a sense of security, stability, and comfort. Whether it is in personal or professional life, loyalty plays a vital role in helping people navigate through tough times. This chapter will explore the importance of loyalty in times of crisis, how to maintain it, the benefits of loyalty in overcoming adversity, examples of loyalty in crisis, the potential risks of losing loyalty, and effective strategies for rebuilding it after a crisis.

The Importance of Loyalty in Times of Crisis

In times of crisis, loyalty can be the difference between survival and failure. It is a quality that helps people persevere through difficult times and overcome challenges. When faced with a crisis, individuals and organizations need to rely on their support networks to help them weather the storm. Loyalty helps build a sense of community and fosters a supportive environment that can help individuals and organizations get through tough times. It is the glue that binds people together in times of crisis.

The Importance of Loyalty in Times of Crisis

Maintaining loyalty in difficult situations requires effort and dedication. It is important to establish strong relationships with people, so they feel valued and supported. Building trust and fostering a sense of belonging are critical to maintaining loyalty. Communication is also key to

LOYALTY IN CRISIS

maintaining loyalty. It is essential to keep people informed of what is happening and to provide regular updates. This helps build transparency and fosters trust. In difficult situations, it is also important to be proactive in addressing issues and providing support. This shows that people are valued and that their needs are being considered. Providing support and showing empathy are key to maintaining loyalty in difficult situations.

The Benefits of Loyalty in Overcoming Adversity

Loyalty has many benefits in overcoming adversity. One of the primary benefits of loyalty is that it fosters a sense of community and support. When people feel supported and valued, they are more likely to persevere through difficult times. Loyalty also helps build resilience. When people know that they have a support network, they are better equipped to deal with challenges and setbacks. Loyalty also fosters a sense of belonging, which can be crucial in times of crisis. When people feel like they are part of a community, they are more likely to work together and support each other.

Examples of Loyalty in Crisis in Personal and Professional Life

There are many examples of loyalty in crisis in personal and professional life. In personal life, loyalty can be seen in the way families come together to support each other in times of crisis. Whether it is an illness, a death, or a financial setback, families often rally around each other to provide support and comfort. In professional life, loyalty can be seen in the way colleagues come together to support each other during challenging times. Whether it is a project deadline, a difficult client, or a company crisis, colleagues often work together to overcome challenges and provide support.

LOYALTY IN CRISIS

The Potential Risks of Losing Loyalty in Times of Crisis

To maintain loyalty in the face of competition, employees must remain objective and fair. This means avoiding taking sides or showing favoritism and being willing to recognize and support the contributions and accomplishments of all colleagues and superiors, regardless of personal preferences. Additionally, employees can maintain loyalty by focusing on their own work and performance, rather than getting caught up in office politics or gossip.

Effective Strategies for Rebuilding Loyalty after Crisis

Rebuilding loyalty after a crisis requires effort and dedication. The first step in rebuilding loyalty is to acknowledge the issue and take responsibility for any mistakes that were made. It is important to communicate openly and transparently with people and to listen to their concerns. This helps rebuild trust and shows that people's needs are being considered. Providing support and showing empathy are also crucial in rebuilding loyalty. This can include offering resources, providing training, or simply being available to listen and offer support. It is also important to demonstrate commitment to change and to take action to address any underlying issues. This helps show that the organization or individual is serious about rebuilding trust and maintaining loyalty.

Another effective strategy for rebuilding loyalty is to focus on building relationships. This can involve reaching out to people individually and taking the time to understand their needs and concerns. Building relationships helps establish trust and fosters a sense of community. It is also important to be proactive in addressing issues and providing support. This helps demonstrate a commitment to the well-being of others and shows that their needs are being considered.

LOYALTY IN CRISIS

In some cases, rebuilding loyalty may require making changes to the way things are done. This may involve revisiting policies or procedures that are causing issues, or making changes to the way that communication is handled. It is important to be open to feedback and to make changes where necessary to address any underlying issues.

Conclusion

In conclusion, loyalty is a crucial element in times of crisis. It helps build a sense of community, fosters resilience, and supports individuals and organizations in overcoming adversity. Maintaining loyalty requires effort and dedication, but the benefits are significant. Losing loyalty can have significant consequences, but effective strategies can be used to rebuild it. By acknowledging issues, demonstrating commitment to change, building relationships, and providing support, individuals and organizations can rebuild loyalty and emerge stronger from times of crisis.

CHAPTER 16
The Intersection of Loyalty and Ethics

"When loyalty becomes a way of life, success becomes a natural byproduct."

#LOYALTYINEVERYTHING

CHAPTER 16
The Intersection of Loyalty and Ethics

Introduction

The concepts of loyalty and ethics are often seen as conflicting ideals, particularly in situations where one's personal or professional loyalties may come into conflict with their ethical obligations. In Chapter 16, the authors explore the intersection of loyalty and ethics, discussing the importance of ethical considerations in loyalty, how to navigate loyalty in ethically complex situations, the potential risks and benefits of loyalty in ethical decision-making, the role of integrity in loyalty, examples of successful loyalty in ethically challenging scenarios, and the potential consequences of compromising ethics for loyalty.

Importance of Ethical Considerations in Loyalty

Loyalty is often seen as a positive trait, reflecting commitment, devotion, and dedication. However, when loyalty conflicts with ethical considerations, it can lead to serious problems. For instance, an employee may feel loyalty to their boss and their company, but if they witness unethical behavior, their loyalty may lead them to remain silent rather than reporting the wrongdoing. This can result in harm to others, damage to the company's reputation, and legal repercussions. Therefore, ethical considerations must always be taken into account when navigating loyalty.

Navigating Loyalty in Ethically Complex Situations

In ethically complex situations, navigating loyalty can be particularly challenging. For instance, if an employee discovers that their boss is engaging in unethical behavior but also knows that reporting this behavior could result in harm to the company, they may struggle to

THE INTERSECTION OF LOYALTY AND ETHICS

determine the best course of action. In such cases, it is important to carefully consider the ethical implications of one's actions and to seek guidance from trusted sources, such as a supervisor or an ethics hotline.

Potential Risks and Benefits of Loyalty in Ethical Decision-Making

Loyalty can have both positive and negative effects on ethical decision-making. On the one hand, loyalty can motivate individuals to act in the best interests of their organization or community, even when doing so is difficult or unpopular. On the other hand, loyalty can blind individuals to unethical behavior, leading them to turn a blind eye to wrongdoing or even to engage in unethical behavior themselves. Therefore, it is important to recognize both the potential risks and benefits of loyalty in ethical decision-making.

The role of Integrity in Loyalty

Integrity is a crucial component of loyalty in ethical decision-making. Individuals who act with integrity are more likely to make ethical decisions, even when doing so may be difficult or unpopular. Moreover, individuals with integrity are more likely to inspire trust and loyalty in others, creating a culture of ethical behavior within their organization or community. Therefore, it is important to cultivate a strong sense of integrity in oneself and to promote integrity in others.

Examples of Successful Loyalty in Ethically Challenging Scenarios

There are many examples of successful loyalty in ethically challenging scenarios. For instance, whistleblowers who report wrongdoing within their organization often face significant risks, including retaliation, ostracism, and job loss. However, many whistleblowers are motivated

THE INTERSECTION OF LOYALTY AND ETHICS

by a sense of loyalty to their organization and a desire to protect its reputation and values. Similarly, soldiers who risk their lives in service to their country are often motivated by a sense of loyalty to their comrades and to the ideals of their nation. In such cases, loyalty can inspire individuals to act with courage and integrity, even in the face of great adversity.

Potential Consequences of Compromising Ethics for Loyalty

Compromising ethics for loyalty can have serious consequences. For instance, a doctor who falsifies medical records to protect a colleague may put patients at risk of harm. Similarly, a manager who covers up unethical behavior by a subordinate may damage the company's reputation and expose it to legal liability. Moreover, compromising ethics for loyalty can erode trust and credibility, both within one's organization and in the broader community. Therefore, it is important to recognize the potential consequences of compromising ethics for loyalty and to avoid such behavior whenever possible.

Strategies for Navigating the Intersection of Loyalty and Ethics

Navigating the intersection of loyalty and ethics requires careful consideration and a commitment to integrity. The following strategies can help individuals to make ethical decisions while remaining loyal to their organization or community:

1. Establish clear ethical guidelines: Organizations should establish clear ethical guidelines that provide guidance for ethical decision-making. These guidelines should be communicated clearly and consistently to all employees and should be regularly reviewed and updated as necessary.

2. Encourage reporting of ethical violations: Organizations should encourage employees to report ethical violations without fear of

THE INTERSECTION OF LOYALTY AND ETHICS

retaliation. This can be accomplished through the establishment of an ethics hotline or other reporting mechanism, as well as through the promotion of a culture of transparency and accountability.

3. Foster a culture of integrity: Organizations should foster a culture of integrity by promoting ethical behavior at all levels of the organization. This can be accomplished through the establishment of an ethics committee, training programs for employees, and the inclusion of ethical considerations in performance evaluations.

4. Seek guidance from trusted sources: Individuals should seek guidance from trusted sources, such as a supervisor or an ethics hotline, when facing ethically complex situations. This can help to ensure that decisions are made with integrity and that ethical considerations are taken into account.

Conclusion

The intersection of loyalty and ethics can be challenging to navigate, but it is crucial for individuals and organizations to do so in order to promote ethical behavior and maintain trust and credibility. By establishing clear ethical guidelines, encouraging reporting of ethical violations, fostering a culture of integrity, and seeking guidance from trusted sources, individuals and organizations can navigate the intersection of loyalty and ethics with integrity and responsibility.

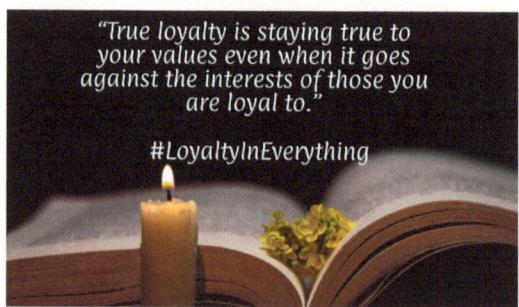

CHAPTER 17
Loyalty in Leadership

"A LOYAL CUSTOMER BASE IS THE LIFELINE OF ANY SUCCESSFUL BUSINESS."

#LOYALTYINEVERYTHING

CHAPTER 17
Loyalty in Leadership

Introduction

Loyalty in leadership is an important aspect of creating and maintaining a healthy organizational culture. Leaders who are loyal to their team members can inspire and motivate them, foster a positive work environment, and build a sense of trust and loyalty within the organization. This, in turn, can lead to increased employee morale, engagement, and productivity. However, loyalty in leadership can also have its pitfalls if not balanced appropriately. In this paper, we will discuss the importance of loyalty in effective leadership, how loyalty can impact organizational culture and employee morale, building loyalty among team members, balancing loyalty to employees with loyalty to the organization, the potential pitfalls of loyalty in leadership, and examples of successful leadership through loyalty.

Importance of Loyalty in Effective Leadership

Loyalty in leadership is essential for effective leadership because it establishes trust and credibility between the leader and the team. When employees feel that their leader is loyal to them, they are more likely to trust and respect them. This trust and respect can lead to increased engagement, collaboration, and productivity, as employees feel more invested in their work and the organization. Additionally, loyalty in leadership can also inspire employees to be loyal to their leader and the organization, creating a sense of community and shared purpose within the workplace.

LOYALTY IN LEADERSHIP

Impact of Loyalty on Organizational Culture and Employee Morale

Loyalty in leadership can have a significant impact on organizational culture and employee morale. When leaders prioritize loyalty, they create a work environment that is supportive, collaborative, and focused on the success of the team as a whole. This can lead to increased employee morale, job satisfaction, and motivation, as employees feel that they are part of a larger community that values their contributions. Additionally, a culture of loyalty can also foster innovation and creativity, as employees feel more comfortable taking risks and sharing their ideas with their colleagues.

Building Loyalty Among Team Members

Building loyalty among team members requires leaders to demonstrate their loyalty through their actions and decisions. This can include things like recognizing and rewarding employees for their hard work, providing opportunities for growth and development, and being transparent and communicative about organizational decisions. Additionally, leaders can also build loyalty by fostering a culture of respect, trust, and collaboration within the team. This can involve creating opportunities for team members to work together, encouraging open and honest communication, and setting clear expectations and goals for the team.

Balancing Loyalty to Employees with Loyalty to the Organization

While loyalty to employees is important, it is also important for leaders to balance this loyalty with loyalty to the organization as a whole. This requires leaders to make difficult decisions that may not always be popular with their team members but are necessary for the success of the organization. For example, leaders may need to make decisions that

LOYALTY IN LEADERSHIP

involve layoffs or budget cuts, even if it means that some team members will be affected. In these situations, it is important for leaders to be transparent and communicative about the reasoning behind their decisions, while also demonstrating empathy and compassion for those affected.

Potential Pitfalls of Loyalty in Leadership

While loyalty in leadership can be beneficial, it can also have its pitfalls if not balanced appropriately. One potential pitfall is that leaders may become too loyal to certain team members, which can lead to favoritism or a lack of accountability. This can create a toxic work environment where some team members feel undervalued or unappreciated. Additionally, leaders may also become too focused on maintaining loyalty at all costs, which can lead to a lack of innovation and a resistance to change. This can be detrimental to the organization's long-term success, as it may prevent the organization from adapting to changing market conditions or embracing new ideas and technologies.

Examples of Successful Leadership through Loyalty

There are many examples of successful leadership through loyalty, both in the business world and beyond. One notable example is the leadership of Howard Schultz, the former CEO of Starbucks. Schultz was known for his loyalty to his employees, whom he referred to as "partners." He believed that investing in his employees' growth and development was key to the company's success. As a result, Starbucks became known for its supportive and collaborative work environment, which fostered a sense of community and loyalty among its employees.

Another example of successful leadership through loyalty is the leadership of Angela Ahrendts, the former CEO of Burberry. Ahrendts

LOYALTY IN LEADERSHIP

was known for her loyalty to the Burberry brand, which she believed was key to the company's success. She also demonstrated her loyalty to her employees by investing in their growth and development, and by fostering a culture of respect and collaboration within the company. Under her leadership, Burberry experienced significant growth and success.

Conclusion

In conclusion, loyalty in leadership is an important aspect of creating and maintaining a healthy organizational culture. Leaders who prioritize loyalty can inspire and motivate their team members, foster a positive work environment, and build a sense of trust and loyalty within the organization. However, it is important for leaders to balance their loyalty to employees with their loyalty to the organization as a whole, and to avoid becoming too focused on maintaining loyalty at all costs. By building loyalty among team members and making difficult decisions when necessary, leaders can create a culture of trust, respect, and collaboration that benefits both employees and the organization as a whole.

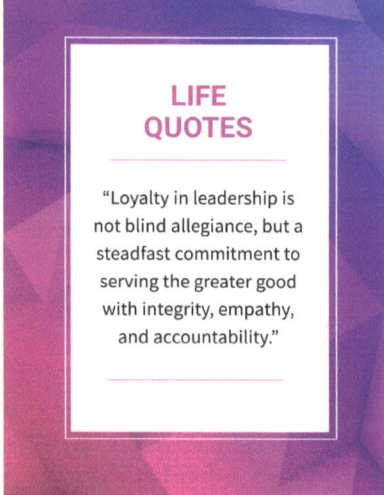

LIFE QUOTES

"Loyalty in leadership is not blind allegiance, but a steadfast commitment to serving the greater good with integrity, empathy, and accountability."

CHAPTER 18
Loyalty in Family Dynamics

"Life's greatest joys are amplified when shared with those who have remained loyal through it all."

#LOYALTYINEVERYTHING

CHAPTER 18
Loyalty in Family Dynamics

Introduction

Loyalty is a critical aspect of family relationships. It is the foundation upon which family bonds are built and maintained. Loyalty involves being devoted to and supportive of family members. Family members who are loyal to one another are there for each other through thick and thin. Loyalty in family dynamics plays an essential role in shaping the family's culture, traditions, and values. In this chapter, we will explore the role of loyalty in family relationships, the challenges of balancing loyalty to family members, building loyalty in blended families, the importance of setting boundaries in family loyalty, maintaining loyalty in the face of family conflict, and examples of successful family loyalty in personal life.

The Role of Loyalty in Family Relationships

Loyalty in family relationships involves a commitment to supporting and standing by family members, even during difficult times. It means being there for each other, celebrating each other's successes, and offering support and encouragement during challenging times. Loyalty is often the glue that holds families together during tough times. Family members who are loyal to one another are more likely to work through problems and find solutions together. They trust one another and feel comfortable being open and honest about their thoughts and feelings.

LOYALTY IN FAMILY DYNAMICS

The Challenges of Balancing Loyalty to Family Members

While loyalty is an essential aspect of family relationships, it can also create challenges. For example, when a family member is in conflict with another family member, balancing loyalty to both individuals can be difficult. A person may feel torn between their loyalty to one family member and their loyalty to another. In such situations, it is essential to navigate the situation with sensitivity, tact, and empathy. It may involve taking a neutral stance and avoiding taking sides.

Building Loyalty in Blended Families

Blended families are families where one or both parents have children from previous relationships. Building loyalty in blended families can be challenging, as family members may have different loyalties and allegiances. To build loyalty in blended families, it is essential to create a sense of unity and belonging. This can be achieved by establishing family traditions, involving all family members in decision-making processes, and creating opportunities for family members to spend quality time together.

The Importance of Setting Boundaries in Family Loyalty

Setting boundaries is essential in maintaining healthy family relationships. In the context of family loyalty, setting boundaries involves defining what behaviors are acceptable and what behaviors are not. It may involve setting limits on how much time and energy a family member is willing to invest in supporting another family member. Setting boundaries is essential to prevent family members from feeling overwhelmed or resentful. It is also important to communicate boundaries clearly and respectfully to avoid causing hurt or misunderstanding.

LOYALTY IN FAMILY DYNAMICS

Maintaining Loyalty in the Face of Family Conflict

Family conflict is a natural part of family dynamics. It can arise due to differences in opinions, values, and beliefs. Maintaining loyalty in the face of family conflict involves finding ways to navigate the situation with empathy, understanding, and respect. It may involve listening to all family members' perspectives, seeking to understand their feelings, and finding common ground. In some cases, maintaining loyalty may involve finding ways to compromise and finding solutions that work for everyone involved.

Examples of Successful Family Loyalty in Personal Life

Successful family loyalty can take many forms. One example is the story of a family who supported their son during his battle with cancer. The family members rallied around the son, providing emotional and practical support during his treatment. They remained loyal to him, even when the situation was challenging, and he needed them the most. The son eventually recovered, and the family's loyalty played a critical role in his recovery.

Another example of successful family loyalty is the story of a couple who supported each other during a difficult time. The couple had been together for many years, and when one of them experienced a serious health issue, the other partner remained devoted and loyal, providing emotional support and practical help during the recovery period. This loyalty strengthened their bond and brought them even closer together.

LOYALTY IN FAMILY DYNAMICS

A third example of successful family loyalty is the story of a family who supported their daughter's decision to pursue her dreams. The daughter had a passion for the arts but faced criticism and doubt from extended family members who believed that pursuing such a career was unrealistic. However, her immediate family remained loyal to her and provided support and encouragement, enabling her to pursue her dreams. The daughter went on to achieve success in her chosen field, and her family's loyalty played a critical role in her success.

Conclusion

Loyalty is a fundamental aspect of family relationships. It involves being committed to and supportive of family members, even during challenging times. Balancing loyalty to family members can be challenging, particularly in the face of family conflict. However, setting boundaries, building unity in blended families, and maintaining loyalty in the face of conflict can help overcome these challenges. Successful family loyalty can take many forms, from supporting a family member during a health crisis to helping them pursue their dreams. Ultimately, family loyalty is essential in maintaining healthy and strong family relationships.

" True loyalty within a family is not measured by blood or obligation, but by the unwavering support, unconditional love, and mutual respect that transcends any challenge or circumstance. "

#LoyaltyInEverything

CHAPTER 19
The Psychology of Loyalty

"LOYALTY IS NOT JUST A VIRTUE; IT'S AN INVESTMENT THAT PAYS DIVIDENDS OVER A LIFETIME."

#LOYALTYINEVERYTHING

CHAPTER 19
The Psychology of Loyalty

Introduction

Loyalty is a complex psychological phenomenon that involves both cognitive and emotional processes. It refers to a strong sense of commitment or devotion towards a person, group, or organization, often characterized by a willingness to make sacrifices and remain faithful even in the face of adversity or temptation. In this chapter, we will explore the cognitive and emotional mechanisms underlying loyalty, the role of attachment theory in understanding loyalty, the potential benefits and risks of loyalty from a psychological perspective, how to recognize unhealthy patterns of loyalty, and examples of successful loyalty from a psychological perspective.

Cognitive and Emotional Mechanisms Behind Loyalty

Loyalty is often seen as a product of both cognitive and emotional processes. From a cognitive perspective, loyalty involves a belief that the object of loyalty (person, group, or organization) is deserving of the loyalty and commitment being offered. This belief is often rooted in a sense of shared values, interests, and experiences between the loyal individual and the object of loyalty. For example, a person may be loyal to a political party because they share the party's values and beliefs.

From an emotional perspective, loyalty involves feelings of attachment, affection, and trust towards the object of loyalty. These feelings are often the result of positive experiences and interactions with the object of loyalty over time. For example, a person may be loyal to a particular brand of clothing because they have had positive experiences with the brand in the past, and they trust the brand to continue to provide high-quality clothing.

THE PSYCHOLOGY OF LOYALTY

The Role of Attachment Theory in Understanding Loyalty

Attachment theory is a psychological theory that explains how humans form close emotional bonds with others. According to attachment theory, the way individuals form these bonds is influenced by their early childhood experiences with primary caregivers. These experiences shape the individual's internal working model of relationships, which in turn affects how they approach and respond to relationships throughout their lives.

Attachment theory can be useful in understanding loyalty because it highlights the importance of emotional bonds and trust in relationships. Individuals who have secure attachment styles are more likely to develop strong, positive relationships that are characterized by loyalty and commitment. In contrast, individuals with insecure attachment styles may struggle to form and maintain these types of relationships.

The Potential Benefits and Risks of Loyalty from a Psychological Perspective

Loyalty can have both potential benefits and risks from a psychological perspective. On the one hand, loyalty can provide a sense of security, belonging, and identity for individuals. Being loyal to a person, group, or organization can help individuals feel like they are part of something larger than themselves, and it can provide a sense of purpose and meaning in their lives. Loyalty can also help to build trust and foster positive relationships with others.

On the other hand, loyalty can also have its risks. Blind loyalty, where individuals remain committed to a person, group, or organization despite evidence of harmful or unethical behavior, can be harmful to

THE PSYCHOLOGY OF LOYALTY

individuals and society as a whole. Blind loyalty can lead to individuals ignoring or excusing harmful behavior, which can perpetuate injustice and harm. Additionally, loyalty can lead to individuals staying in relationships or situations that are harmful or unfulfilling because they feel obligated to remain loyal.

How to Recognize Unhealthy Patterns of Loyalty

It is important to recognize unhealthy patterns of loyalty to avoid harm to oneself and others. Unhealthy patterns of loyalty may include blind loyalty, where individuals remain committed to a person, group, or organization despite evidence of harmful or unethical behavior, and codependency, where individuals prioritize the needs and wants of the object of loyalty over their own well-being. Additionally, individuals may exhibit unhealthy patterns of loyalty when they feel obligated to remain loyal even when the relationship or situation is harmful or unfulfilling.

Recognizing these patterns of loyalty can be difficult, as they may be deeply ingrained in an individual's beliefs and behaviors. However, some signs of unhealthy loyalty may include:

• Ignoring or excusing harmful behavior: Individuals may rationalize or excuse harmful behavior from the object of their loyalty, even if it goes against their own values or beliefs.

• Sacrificing personal well-being: Individuals may prioritize the needs or wants of the object of their loyalty over their own well-being, to the point of neglecting their own needs.

• Feeling trapped: Individuals may feel trapped in a relationship or situation due to a sense of obligation to remain loyal, even if the relationship or situation is harmful or unfulfilling.

THE PSYCHOLOGY OF LOYALTY

• Fear of abandonment: Individuals may fear losing the object of their loyalty, even if it means remaining in a harmful or unfulfilling relationship or situation.

If an individual recognizes these patterns of loyalty in themselves, it may be helpful to seek support from a mental health professional or trusted friend or family member. Working to understand and challenge these patterns of loyalty can be an important step towards building healthier and more fulfilling relationships.

Examples of Successful Loyalty from a Psychological Perspective

While loyalty can have its risks, there are also examples of successful loyalty from a psychological perspective. Successful loyalty involves remaining committed to a person, group, or organization while also maintaining a sense of critical thinking and independent judgment. Successful loyalty can foster positive relationships, build trust, and promote personal growth and fulfillment.

One example of successful loyalty is in close personal relationships, such as romantic partnerships or close friendships. Successful loyalty in these relationships involves remaining committed to the relationship while also maintaining a sense of independence and autonomy. This can involve communicating openly and honestly, respecting each other's boundaries and needs, and supporting each other's personal growth and fulfillment.

Another example of successful loyalty is in organizational contexts, such as loyalty to a company or sports team. Successful loyalty in these contexts involves remaining committed to the organization while also maintaining a sense of critical thinking and independent judgment. This

THE PSYCHOLOGY OF LOYALTY

can involve advocating for positive change within the organization, holding the organization accountable for harmful or unethical behavior, and promoting a culture of integrity and respect.

Conclusion

Loyalty is a complex psychological phenomenon that involves both cognitive and emotional processes. It can provide a sense of security, belonging, and identity for individuals, but it can also have its risks, particularly when it involves blind loyalty or codependency. Recognizing unhealthy patterns of loyalty and working to challenge them can be an important step towards building healthier and more fulfilling relationships. Successful loyalty involves remaining committed to a person, group, or organization while also maintaining a sense of critical thinking and independent judgment. By understanding the psychological mechanisms underlying loyalty, we can work towards fostering positive relationships and promoting personal growth and fulfillment.

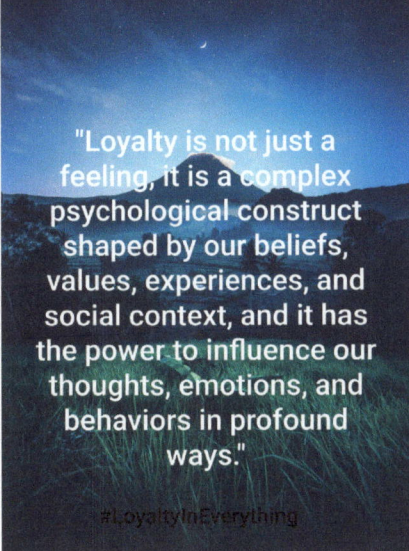

"Loyalty is not just a feeling, it is a complex psychological construct shaped by our beliefs, values, experiences, and social context, and it has the power to influence our thoughts, emotions, and behaviors in profound ways."

#LoyaltyInEverything

The Psychology of Loyalty

CHAPTER 20
Cultivating Loyalty through Gratitude

"THE MEASURE OF TRUE CHARACTER LIES IN THE LOYALTY ONE SHOWS DURING TIMES OF ADVERSITY."

#LOYALTYINEVERYTHING

CHAPTER 20
Cultivating Loyalty through Gratitude

Introduction

Loyalty is a complex psychological phenomenon that involves both cognitive and emotional processes. It refers to a strong sense of commitment or devotion towards a person, group, or organization, often characterized by a willingness to make sacrifices and remain faithful even in the face of adversity or temptation. In this chapter, we will explore the cognitive and emotional mechanisms underlying loyalty, the role of attachment theory in understanding loyalty, the potential benefits and risks of loyalty from a psychological perspective, how to recognize unhealthy patterns of loyalty, and examples of successful loyalty from a psychological perspective.

The Importance of Gratitude in Building Loyalty

Gratitude is a feeling of appreciation and thankfulness for the positive aspects of life. Gratitude involves recognizing and acknowledging the good things in life, no matter how small or big. When we practice gratitude, we cultivate a positive attitude and an optimistic outlook on life. People who practice gratitude tend to be happier, more optimistic, and have better relationships. Therefore, gratitude is an essential ingredient in building loyalty. When we express gratitude towards someone, we show them that we value and appreciate them. This appreciation, in turn, makes the person feel valued, acknowledged, and appreciated, creating a sense of loyalty towards the individual or organization.

Gratitude also helps to build trust, which is an essential component of loyalty. When we express gratitude, we create a sense of trust and

CULTIVATING LOYALTY WITH GRATITUDE

respect between ourselves and others. This trust leads to greater loyalty because people tend to remain loyal to those they trust. For instance, when a boss expresses gratitude towards an employee for a job well done, the employee feels valued and appreciated, creating a sense of trust and loyalty towards the boss. Therefore, cultivating gratitude is an essential aspect of building loyalty.

How to Express Gratitude to Cultivate Loyalty

Expressing gratitude is not just about saying thank you. It involves recognizing the effort, time, and resources that someone has put into a particular task or relationship. The following are some tips on how to express gratitude to cultivate loyalty:

1. Be Specific: When expressing gratitude, be specific about what you are grateful for. Instead of just saying thank you, mention the specific action that you are grateful for. For example, instead of saying, "Thank you for your help," say, "Thank you for taking the time to help me with my project. Your expertise and support were invaluable."

2. Be Sincere: Express gratitude genuinely and sincerely. When expressing gratitude, ensure that your words and tone convey your sincerity. People can easily tell when gratitude is not genuine, which can have the opposite effect of what you intend.

3. Show Appreciation: Show appreciation by taking the time to thank people personally. A personal thank-you note, email, or phone call goes a long way in showing appreciation.

4. Be Timely: Express gratitude in a timely manner. Don't wait too long to show appreciation, as the moment may pass. The longer you wait, the less impactful your gratitude will be.

CULTIVATING LOYALTY WITH GRATITUDE

5. Be Consistent: Express gratitude consistently. Don't wait for special occasions to show appreciation. Make it a habit to express gratitude regularly, as this helps to create a culture of gratitude.

The Impact of Gratitude on Personal and Professional Relationships

Gratitude has a profound impact on personal and professional relationships. The following are some of the ways that gratitude impacts relationships:

1. Increases Happiness: Gratitude increases happiness, both in the person expressing gratitude and the person receiving it. When we feel appreciated and valued, we tend to be happier.

2. Enhances Well-being: Gratitude enhances well-being. People who practice gratitude tend to have better physical and mental health, better sleep, and lower levels of stress.

3. Improves Communication: Gratitude improves communication by fostering positive feelings and creating a sense of trust between individuals. This trust leads to better communication, as people feel comfortable sharing their thoughts and ideas.

4. Builds Trust: Gratitude builds trust, which is essential in any relationship. When we express gratitude, we create a sense of trust and respect between ourselves and others, leading to greater loyalty.

5. Strengthens Relationships: Gratitude strengthens relationships by creating a sense of connection and belonging. When we express gratitude towards someone, we are acknowledging their value and worth, strengthening the bond between us.

CULTIVATING LOYALTY WITH GRATITUDE

Building a Culture of Gratitude to Foster Loyalty

Building a culture of gratitude is essential in fostering loyalty in any organization or relationship. The following are some tips on how to build a culture of gratitude:

1. Lead by Example: Leaders should lead by example by expressing gratitude regularly. When leaders show appreciation towards their employees, it creates a culture of gratitude that cascades down to the entire organization.

2. Make Gratitude a Habit: Make gratitude a habit by incorporating it into daily routines. For instance, starting meetings with a gratitude exercise or having a gratitude journal at the office can help to cultivate a culture of gratitude.

3. Celebrate Wins: Celebrate wins and successes by acknowledging the effort and hard work put into achieving them. This not only shows gratitude but also motivates individuals to continue putting in the effort.

4. Encourage Feedback: Encourage feedback from employees and colleagues, and express gratitude for their input. This feedback not only helps to improve the organization but also creates a culture of open communication and gratitude.

5. Incorporate Gratitude into Performance Evaluations: Incorporate gratitude into performance evaluations by acknowledging the positive contributions made by employees. This not only shows appreciation but also creates a sense of loyalty towards the organization.

CULTIVATING LOYALTY WITH GRATITUDE

Examples of Successful Gratitude Practices in Cultivating Loyalty

The following are some examples of successful gratitude practices in cultivating loyalty:

1. Zappos: Zappos is an online shoe and clothing store that is known for its customer service. One of the ways that Zappos fosters loyalty is by encouraging employees to show gratitude towards customers. Zappos encourages employees to write personal thank-you notes to customers, creating a sense of appreciation and loyalty towards the company.

2. Starbucks: Starbucks is known for its customer loyalty program, which rewards customers for their loyalty. One of the ways that Starbucks fosters loyalty is by showing gratitude towards its customers through personalized rewards, such as free drinks and discounts.

3. Google: Google fosters loyalty by expressing gratitude towards its employees. Google offers its employees perks, such as free meals, massages, and onsite medical care, showing appreciation for their hard work and dedication.

4. Southwest Airlines: Southwest Airlines is known for its customer service and employee loyalty. Southwest fosters loyalty by expressing gratitude towards its employees through recognition programs, such as the "Spirit of Customer Service" award, which acknowledges employees who go above and beyond in providing excellent customer service.

CULTIVATING LOYALTY WITH GRATITUDE

Conclusion

Gratitude is a powerful tool that has the potential to transform relationships, organizations, and well-being. Gratitude fosters loyalty by creating a sense of trust, respect, and appreciation between individuals. To cultivate loyalty through gratitude, it is important to be specific, sincere, show appreciation, be timely, and be consistent in expressing gratitude. Gratitude has a profound impact on personal and professional relationships, enhancing happiness, well-being, communication, trust, and strengthening relationships. Building a culture of gratitude is essential in fostering loyalty in any organization or relationship. Successful gratitude practices, such as those employed by Zappos, Starbucks, Google, and Southwest Airlines, show the impact of gratitude on loyalty and demonstrate how organizations can foster loyalty through gratitude.

In conclusion, cultivating loyalty through gratitude requires intentionality, consistency, and authenticity. By expressing gratitude regularly and building a culture of gratitude, individuals and organizations can foster loyalty and strengthen relationships. Gratitude is a simple yet powerful tool that has the potential to transform lives, organizations, and society as a whole. It is important to cultivate gratitude in our daily lives, not only for our own well-being but also for the well-being of those around us. As the saying goes, "Gratitude turns what we have into enough." Let us cultivate gratitude and foster loyalty in our personal and professional relationships, making the world a better place, one expression of gratitude at a time.

> "Loyalty is not just earned through rewards or promises, but by the genuine appreciation and gratitude we show towards those who stand by us. Cultivate loyalty with the fertilizer of gratitude, and watch it blossom into a garden of unwavering devotion."

Check out the advertisement section

THANK YOU FOR READING AND SUPPORTING
LOYALTY IN EVERYTHING:
A GUIDE TO BUILDING STRONG
RELATIONSHIPS IN BUSINESS AND LIFE

Scan Here:
Or Go To The Following Link:
https://poplme.co/hash/pkRc45gn/1/share

Loyalty In Everything

Loyalty & Friends

Self-Love Podcast

Loyalty is a dynamic and compassionate host who brings a wealth of knowledge and experience to the Loyalty & Friends Self-Love Podcast. Her mission is to empower and inspire her listeners to cultivate self-love and positive relationships in their lives.

Each episode of the Loyalty & Friends Self-Love Podcast features insightful conversations with thought leaders, experts, and real people who share their unique perspectives and experiences. From practical tips for building self-esteem to strategies for strengthening friendships and romantic relationships, Loyalty offers a wealth of wisdom and guidance for listeners.

If you're looking to improve your mental health, build stronger relationships with others, or simply learn more about the power of self-love, the Loyalty & Friends Self-Love Podcast is the perfect resource. Tune in to join the conversation and discover the tools you need to live your best life.

Scan Here:
Or Go To The Following Link:
Erickallenrecovery.com

Exclusively on Amazon:

ANALYZE THI$

Erick Allen or EA as we know him is a Certified Alcohol & Drug Abuse Counselor. His mission in life is to lift others through the diagnosis and treatment of addiction and mental illness.
Resiliency and Recovery - One individual, One family, and One community at a time

State Credentials and Licensure (Oregon):
Certified Alcohol & Drug Counselor (CADC)
Qualified Mental Health Associate (QMHA)
Registered under the National Provider Identifier Database
B.A. in Sociology

Being driven and committed to advocating for hood very own family have inspired him to support and share healing strategies with others

His most recent accomplishment is his most recent publication the Affirmations for Recovery journal. This journal is designed to guide others through recovery from life trauma through the practice of Affirmations.

Everyone has a story to tell.
We want to hear yours!

Scan QR Code to purchase book

MASUN JARZZ ALL WALKS OF LIFE ALL CORNERS OF THE EARTH!

INVEST IN YOURSELF today and become a Co~author for only $500! Books are included.

Become apart of this life changing global phenomenon anthology series!

Minimize your empowering story into 1,500-2,000 words. This is a great opportunity to positively impact, empower and truly inspire the entire world, while making endless money!

Refer a friend or family member and you will receive $25.

Contact Information:
1 {559}~5~MJARZZ
1 {559}~565~2799
www.illusionmasunjarzz.com

NOW OFFERING FINANCING THROUGH:
AFTER PAY
KLARNA
AFFIRM
ZIP

Author
TénéNi Mason
Marquis Who's Who Top Artist August 2022

Daily Affirmations From The Lord's Prayer
Devotional Meditation
Prayer Book

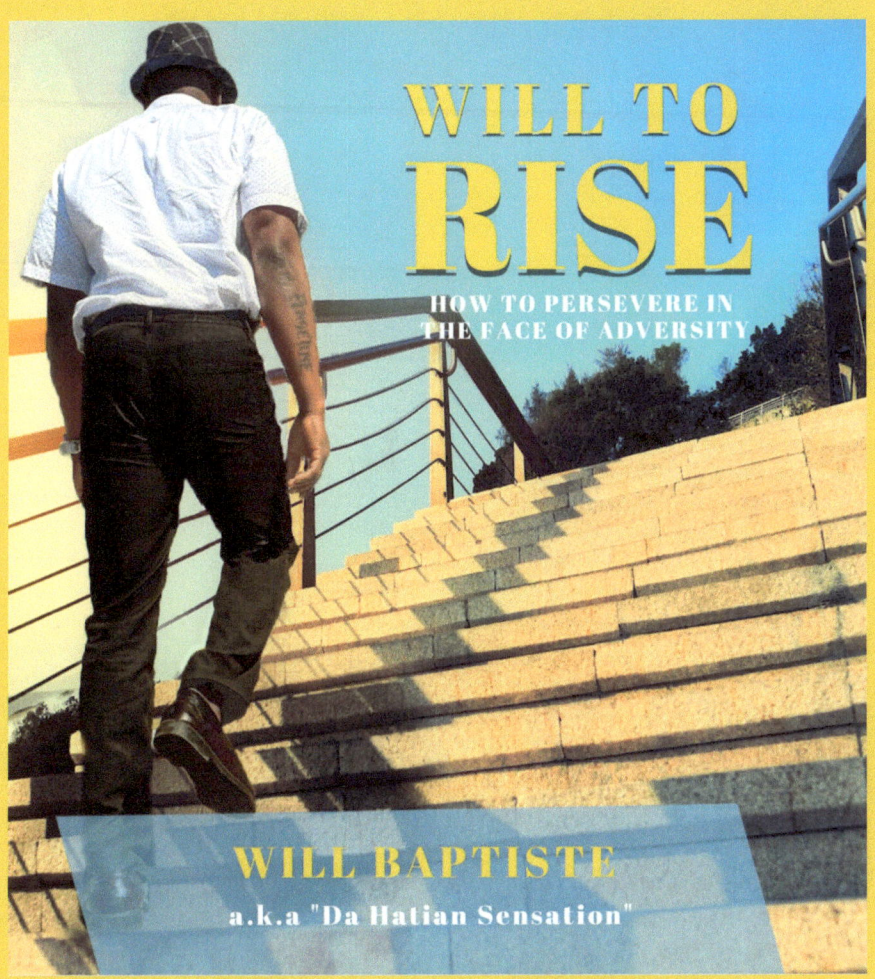

WILL BAPTISTE IS A FAITH-BASED COACH, HE LIVES IN MONTREAL. HE IS A CERTIFIED MENTAL HEALTH FIRST AID BY THE MENTAL HEALTH COMMISSION OF CANADA) AND HE IS ALSO A PODCAST HOST (WILL TO RISE) AND A PUBLIC SPEAKER

ASK HIM ABOUT:
E-MOTIONAL MASTERY
E-MOTIONAL FREEDOM CONSCIOUS PARENTING RELATIONSHIP WITH ONESELF .

STAY TUNED FOR HIS BOOK RELEASE WILL TO RISE SOON.

MEETWILLTORISE.COM

www.ingramcontent.com/pod-product-compliance
Lightning Source LLC
Chambersburg PA
CBHW041611220426
43669CB00001B/3